7

PRINCIPLES OF

TRANSFORMATIONAL

LEADERSHIP

CREATE A MINDSET OF PASSION, INNOVATION, AND GROWTH

HUGH BLANE

CAREER
PRESS

7 PRINCIPLES OF TRANSFORMATIONAL LEADERSHIP
TYPESET BY PERFECTYPE, NASHVILLE, TENN.
Cover design by Jonathan Bush Design
Printed in the U.S.A.

To order this title, please call toll-free 1-800-CAREER-1 (NJ and Canada: 201-848-0310) to order using VISA or MasterCard, or for further information on books from Career Press.

CAREER
PRESS

The Career Press, Inc.
12 Parish Drive
Wayne, NJ 07470
www.careerpress.com

Library of Congress Cataloging-in-Publication Data

CIP Data Available Upon Request.

ACKNOWLEDGMENTS

The acknowledgment section of a book is not written for the reader. It is for the author to thank the people who helped him or her on the journey of writing a book. Indulge me as I thank a group of very special people.

First and foremost I want to say thank you to my parents. Both were courageous souls who chose to immigrate with two small children from Scotland to Canada and then Birmingham, Alabama, in 1968. Were it not for their desire for a better life, for themselves and primarily for their children, this book would not be in your hands. Both would be exceptionally proud of this accomplishment, as I am of theirs.

I want to thank my mentor and business advisor Alan Weiss. Alan has stretched my thinking and, by doing so, enriched my life in ways I never imagined possible. Thank you, Alan, for showing me how to live boldly, confidently, and generously. And yes, the second book is on its way.

To the clients who partnered with me to convert their human potential into accelerated results I cannot thank you enough. You gave me the opportunity to bring the insights of transformational leadership into your all-too-often overwhelmed, overscheduled, and overbooked workplace and to make a difference in your performance while also enabling human flourishing. I am enriched by your partnership and thank you.

I want to thank the business colleagues who positively shaped my thinking with the book. A heartfelt thank you goes out to Roberta Matuson, Linda Popky, Mark Rodgers, Judy Chan, and Richard Citrin. Each of you inspired me to become an author and to get out of my own way with my writing. I am honored to join you as published authors and indebted to you for your support and encouragement.

Thank you to my sister, Elise, who sees the very best in me and knew I had a book to write even when I didn't. Your belief in me is without question a gift that I cherish and relied heavily upon while writing the book. To my best man, Robert, your wisdom, faith, and discernment have shaped me in powerful ways. Your thoughts and perspectives are on many pages of this book, and no, you cannot have a portion of the royalties. To my brother from another mother, John Felkins. We became fast friends and your friendship and encouragement have been ballast when I've felt as though I was sinking amidst the responsibilities of work and business. You are a fabulous father and amazing advisor and I am blessed to call you my friend.

Thank you to Adonis McNeal. You've been on the receiving end of far too many calls during which I thought out loud about each of the seven principles and ended up on my soapbox. You were always gracious and generous with your attention and encouragement. You too are my brother from another mother. It's too bad I didn't get your dashing good looks though.

And last, but certainly not least, to the love of my life, Alyson Sharron. Without question, in front of every good man stands a strong, powerful, and loving woman pulling him into the future. You are that for me. I thank you for your swift kick in the pants, your swift voice of encouragement, and the unquestioning admonition of greater possibility. Were it not for you this book would never have happened. Thank you for your patience, love, and support.

CONTENTS

CONTENTS

INTRODUCTION: MINDSET IS NOT JUST FOR ATHLETES, ACADEMICS, AND CAVE-DWELLING MYSTICS

Understand Your Mindset and You'll Understand Your Results

I did not come into this world with an "I can do anything" mindset. Far from it. At 48 years old, I found myself unfulfilled emotionally, spiritually, and financially—in spite of being in the third year of a marriage to the love of my life. I had been working my tail off to be successful, but felt as though I was driving with one foot jammed on the accelerator and the other squarely on the brakes. I was exerting a massive amount of energy each day, but going nowhere fast. Every day I felt like Sisyphus climbing a mountain—only to be rolled back down to the bottom and admonished for daring to climb the mountain. Living this way was exhausting.

In hindsight, my mindset was rooted in scarcity and poverty. No matter what I accomplished, it wasn't good enough. My favorite reply to people giving me compliments and acknowledging me for what I was accomplishing was, "Yes, but. . . ." I summarily dismissed people because I didn't believe what I was accomplishing was up to the high standards I had set. My thinking was my biggest enemy. How did I get here?

On a day like any other for a 6 year old, I was playing in my bedroom when I heard my mother screaming. I ran downstairs and saw her blocking the doorway to our house and three men standing on our front steps. I ran and stood in the cradle of my mother's arm and looked at the men with fear and confusion. They were not police officers delivering bad news about my father, nor were they thugs there to rob us. They were just men doing their job, which on that day was to repossess our furniture. And doing their job left my mother screaming and frantically telephoning my father to "Take care of this!"

During a recession in the 1960s in Scotland, repossessing furniture happened to other families, not to my mother. Christobel Rice Blane had married into one of the wealthiest families in Glasgow, Scotland. Life was exactly as she hoped until my grandfather died. My grandfather, David Blane, was an extraordinarily gifted businessman who started his business life pushing a large wooden cart up and down the streets of Glasgow, offering bread, fruit, fish, and any other product he could sell for a profit. He worked long, hard days and had an "I will do this" mindset.

In the time span of 40 years, my grandfather amassed a fortune. He had a Jaguar, MG, and Rolls Royce dealership, a scrap metal business, and a bookie joint. He raised his 10 children with silver spoons in their mouths and with the support of two nannies. The family home was built and named for a vacation property my grandfather found in Padua, Italy, and had not one, but two, billiard rooms. At one point, my father's clothes were custom tailored and he drove one of the nicest cars in town. My father was the proverbial "big guy on campus."

My mother came from the opposite side of the tracks. Her father was a laborer, who at one time worked in a coal mine. Their family had no money. When my mother was in high school, she had one dress she would wear to school every day. She would come home and iron it to wear again the following day. Cristobel knew she was poor and the thought that kept her motivated was the hope of "getting out of this godforsaken place" and making a better life for herself.

On one hand, the mindset with which my father was raised was one of affluence and privilege. My mother's mindset, on the other hand, was one of poverty and scarcity. What happened on the day the repo men arrived galvanized my mother's mindset and obliterated that of my father. For my mother, the highest hopes she had for her life came crashing down around her. For my father, any sense of self-worth or self-esteem shriveled like a raisin in the sun.

What does this have to do with me and my mindset? On that fateful day, my mindset as a 6 year old shifted from safety and security to fear and uncertainty. I came to believe that whatever possessions I had could and would be taken away from me. This mindset permeated my thinking; my perceptions of people, places, and leadership placed me squarely on track for the life I found myself living at 48 years old.

My intent in recounting this story is to provide you with context about how mindsets and the leadership you and I exhibit are the byproduct of nature as well as nurture. The only real choice we have is to acknowledge our current mindset, accept our role in creating or tolerating it, articulate the desired mindset we want to have, and then take action each day to create it.

I've found that 80 percent of a leader's success is mental. There are leaders who believe that work is a long, slow slog through enemy territory on their belly with bullets flying over their heads. This mindset will produce lower performance 100 percent of the time. You cannot perform at the highest levels if your mindset is equally not at the highest level.

Although neuroscience and psychology have positively shaped my mindset, they are not the cornerstones of this book. I am not a psychologist, but rather a leadership expert who has successfully changed my own mindset, as well as the mindsets of my clients, for the better.

I wrote this book for two key reasons: First, in the world of work, the amount of untapped human potential inside organizations is staggering. After working in 43 states and seven countries on three continents, I've witnessed firsthand 65 percent of employees with a chronic case of JDTM: just doing the minimum. Their mindsets are characterized as exerting the minimum amount of effort possible while maintaining a positive annual review. But before you conclude that employees with JDTM are greedy, lazy, and selfish, consider the fact that leaders in corporations across all industries suffer from JDTM also and are the carriers of the JDTM virus. Far too often, the mission, vision, and values guiding organizations, teams, and individual employees are written by senior leaders while on executive retreats in mountain lodges. They are, in turn, devoid of any tangible connection with the people who meet and engage the customer on a daily basis. Employees suffer from JDTM because their leaders are unwilling to undertake the individual transformations required in order to transform their teams or organizations.

Second, on a personal level, I hope to enable more human flourishing. I believe in the biblical passage that reads, "And to whomsoever much is given, of him shall much be required." I have an obligation and responsibility to take what I've learned and pass it along to others who can benefit. We will cover this in extended detail in the following chapters.

Before moving on, I have an assessment you'll want to complete. These are not ethereal, navel-gazing questions that require you to sit on a cushion in a cross-legged position for 60 minutes. They are statements that, when considered thoughtfully and purposefully, will help you see the connection between your mindset and your results.

The Transformational Leadership Assessment

On a scale from 1 to 10 (1 is strongly disagree and 10 is strongly agree), rate yourself on the following statements:

1. I have a clearly articulated purpose for my leadership and personal life.
2. I have clearly defined the priorities that are in service of my purpose, as well as the people who matter most to me.
3. I have made non-negotiable promises to all of the people who matter most to me both personally and professionally.
4. I know with certainty and have articulated the behaviors I will exhibit in order to achieve my purpose, promises, and priorities.
5. I actively stretch my leadership every year with new projects that provide increased value to the people who matter most to me.
6. I have a remarkable ability to persevere in the face of adversity and setbacks.
7. I actively teach and mentor others in order to cement my learning, as well as to help others grow and learn.

8. When it comes to my thinking, I "play to win" as opposed to "play not to lose."
9. I have cultivated a positive mindset, as well as positive self-talk.
10. I have a contagious and persuasive belief about helping others grow their leadership and enhance their mindset.
11. I praise myself for things I do well and eliminate or reduce the things I don't do well daily, weekly, and monthly.
12. I take time to reflect and think creatively and strategically about my professional and personal life.

After completing the Transformational Leadership Assessment, consider the following questions:

- What statements received the highest and lowest scores?
- What are the implications for these areas being rated so high and low?
- If you could significantly improve one answer, which one would have the biggest positive impact on your leadership and your result?

A Mindset of Growth, Optimism, and Positivity

Here's what I've learned working with organizations such as Sony Pictures, Boeing, Nordstrom, Starbucks, and Microsoft: Transformational leaders are dissatisfied with being good, and instead believe in and strive for a state best described as "flourishing." In this chapter, I start by presenting a new mindset about rethinking the world of work and position you for transformational growth.

If you want a flourishing business—a business that has top-line growth, greater profitability, high levels of customer satisfaction, and top talent retention—you must have flourishing relationships with your employees. In today's world of work, the customer experience must be so compelling that customers would not consider going elsewhere. That can only be created by committed and happy employees.

When leaders commit to creating experiences that are compelling, noteworthy, and loyalty-centric, the only way to execute and deliver this strategy is through happy and satisfied employees. In no uncertain terms, if you want to create a compelling, flourishing experience for your customers but your employees are not flourishing, there is just no way for your business to flourish. The following is an equation that will transform your leadership and your results:

$$FB = (FE + FC + ME)$$

A flourishing business (FB) comes from flourishing employees (FE), flourishing customers (FC), and memorable experiences (ME).

Flourishing employees are created by flourishing leaders who commit to cultivating flourishing customers and producing memorable experiences. And yet, there are employees who should *never* be placed in customer-facing roles but find themselves there on a regular basis. Some of these people are so uncomfortable, incompetent, or indifferent to the customer that they should never be put in roles that require customer interactions.

Are there examples inside your organization in which unhappy employees are creating negative experiences for customers? Are there times when employees see a customer as an interruption and something to be tolerated, as opposed to a precious asset that needs to be cultivated and treated with respect? Is it ever acceptable in your employees' eyes to be rude and uncaring? If you answer yes, the problem doesn't rest with the front-line employee. The bigger question is: Do leaders walk through your doors each morning with a keen desire to make a meaningful difference in your customers' and employees' lives?

If you as a leader have lost this desire and are unable to feel enthused about making a difference in your most important constituents' life, it is time to make an exit from the ranks of leadership. It is really quite simple. If you are not flourishing at work, it is time for a change—first in mindset and then in role, if need be. Your level of personal flourishing permeates and shapes your leadership and shows up in the customer experience.

It's Not What Others Tell You; It's What You Tell Yourself

The number-one lament of readers of my blog is that they feel overwhelmed and don't have the time necessary to effectively lead. This feeling can happen for a variety of reasons, some of which are valid, whereas others are rooted in the leader's mindset. Throughout the last 25 years, I've found six factors that contribute to the feeling of overwhelm—all of which create a mindset that lowers performance and stifles the well-being of customers and employees.

1. **Underperformance is tolerated.** Every organization has employees that underperform and others that over perform. The former are interested in having a paycheck and have little enthusiasm for increasing their performance. Rather than find a job at which the expectations are lower, they're allowed to stay in their roles even in the face of underperformance. When underperformance is tolerated, a clear message is sent to all employees that this is acceptable and there are no repercussions. This mindset stalls growth and is a catalyst for even greater underperformance.

2. **Miscommunication.** When leaders feel overwhelmed and are continually running from one meeting to another without any margin or white space, miscommunication is

assured. By that I mean you will miss the subtle nuances of interpersonal communication, and in the process of rushing from meeting to meeting, miscommunicate expectations due to the anxiety of needing to be in two places at once. This leads to false starts and the all-too-familiar rework required as a result of miscommunication.

3. **Being tired, worn down, and burned out.** In America, leaders pride themselves on pushing themselves to the limit. It is a badge of honor to say to family and friends that you work 70 hours a week. And yet, in study after study, the research shows that as the number of hours you work each week goes up, the quality of your work goes down. Greater effectiveness comes from leaders and employees who are energized, uplifted, and enthused about making a positive difference in the life of a customer. This is nearly impossible to do when a leader or employee is hanging on for dear life and trying to keep their nose above water.

4. **Not having the skills to manage stress effectively.** There are two types of stress we face at one time or another: eustress and distress. Eustress occurs when the gap between what we want and what we have is slightly

pushed, but not in ways that lead us to feel overwhelmed. We see this stress as manageable and our goal achievable.

Distress is the opposite. The gap is unmanageable and the goal is seen as unreachable. This leads us to feel overwhelmed, out of control, and ineffective. Leaders need the ability to capitalize on eustress, as well as the ability to reduce or eliminate the causes and or effects of distress. And yet the number-one strategy for dealing with stress in organizations today is to put your nose to the grindstone and gut it out. There are times when this strategy is needed and the preferred way forward. However, too often working harder is preferred by busy and overwhelmed leaders over working smarter.

5. **Poor time management and priority-setting habits.** The exigency of a leader's day-to-day work is one in which continual priority-setting is a necessity but not a reality. Being able to strategically and respectfully say no to bosses as well as customers is a key skill transformational leaders have mastered. When leaders look at their calendars and ask what percent of their time is spent in low-value producing activities relative to their most strategic priorities, what figure would you expect to hear? Eighty percent? Seventy?

Fifty? All too often the figure from my coaching and consulting clients is 30 percent. With greater priority-setting skills, as well as good time management, a leader can increase the strategic use of their calendar by 25 to 50 percent, which has a transformational impact on their performance.

6. **Unaware of the importance of mindset on performance.** In business schools across the country, the number of classes taught on mindset and mental training is tiny. Yes, psychology is taught in broad and often theoretical terms, much like the tried-and-true courses on financial management and marketing, and new courses on social media.

What happens in between the ears of leaders and employees is in many ways what determines financial performance, market share, and talent acquisition and retention. When a factor as important as mindset is missing from a leader's arsenal of tools, the results are less than appealing.

When you look at this list, undoubtedly you will be able to add other factors that lead you to feel overwhelmed. Just about all of these can be influenced by a leader. Happy employees are essential for happy customers. One of a leader's primary jobs is to manage the mindset of his or her employees so the mindset of the customer is favorable and inclined to do more business with the organization.

How employees talk to themselves is critical. Some may feel that no matter how good an idea they create, management will never support them. If their belief and self-talk is rooted in defeatist language and beliefs, it is impossible to behave differently until what they tell themselves changes.

For example, Robert was a new coaching client in the healthcare field. He told me, as many of my clients do, of the 70-plus hours he was working and the demands on his time. He lamented feeling overwhelmed and frustrated because his day was spent in reactive firefighting mode. Things had gotten so bad that his employees had even asked him to become less reactive and to help them do the same. When I asked who was in charge of his schedule and how he spent his day, his answer was a resolute "hospitals and patients."

Robert was right in one regard: His work was determined in many ways by the ravages of a career in healthcare, where a person's life and well-being is influenced by his or her caregivers. These professions are surrounded by "a decision must be made now circumstances."

But Robert also missed a crucial distinction. Although the external factors influencing his day were real, his response to them was equally so. Robert was not in charge of what happened *to him* every day, but he was certainly in charge of *how he responded* to what happened to him. How Robert responded rested squarely in the six inches separating his two ears. It wasn't his boss, his hospital, or his patients. Robert's mindset was in charge of the people, processes, and perspectives he brought to bear every day. Changing your mindset so as to unleash your human potential is what this book is about.

The good news is there are seven principles that will help you master your leadership mindset and convert your human potential, as well as the potential in your team and organization, into accelerated performance. Each of the following chapters corresponds with a different principle.

1

The Purpose Principle

The One Idea, Dream, Hope, or Aspiration

Ask 10 people what they would do if they won the lottery and had the financial resources to no longer work, and you'll hear ideas such as "start my own business" or "start a charity." Throughout the last 11 years as a financial advisor, I saw this type of wishful thinking. Whenever I met a new or prospective client I would ask a simple, straightforward question: "What, to you, is important about money?" The number-one answer I heard was "security." And on numerous occasions I heard from female clients that they didn't want to end up as a "bag lady."

What was interesting is that the people I was speaking to and meeting with were not financially insecure. They had resources, but still carried with them a poverty mindset. One healthcare executive making more than one million dollars per year was worried about having enough money to retire.

But, having security as a purpose puts a stranglehold on many of the ideas, hopes, and dreams for what our lives can be. The hopes and dreams we have for our lives get pushed aside because of our prevailing mindset.

Let's be clear about the one primary benefit of clarifying your leadership purpose: The jumping-off point for greatness both individually and organizationally is a clear and compelling purpose. People at work or in your personal life who have achieved something extraordinary or who live lives defined as "rewarding" and "uplifting" have a clear and compelling idea about what is important to them, why it is important, and what value they will achieve by working to accomplish it.

One of my clients is a hospital CEO who defined her purpose as follows: "I want to create a culture where every single employee is engaged in creating the extraordinary in patient care and safety." Her purpose translates three things that are important to her:

1. Patient care and safety are paramount.
2. Every employee must be engaged in order to make this happen.
3. Creating the extraordinary is essential.

This CEO is not content with the ordinary. She believes the extraordinary is possible and sees her job as primarily focused on creating the cultural transformation to make this happen. Her purpose guides her every move and permeates her thinking even in the constantly shifting market that is healthcare.

When I asked her about our work together she said, "Getting clear about my purpose was not easy, but it has made leading so much easier and rewarding now that I have it."

That leaves me with these questions for you: Are you clear about your leadership purpose? Do you feel passionate about what you want? Are you relentless in learning and growing your own skill set as a leader as well as your mindset, and creating value for others? Or does each day feel as though you are driving in fog?

What does driving in fog look like from a leadership perspective? Imagine you're on vacation, driving to Napa Valley wine country to taste some of America's most notable wines. In the hopes of making your trip even more memorable you rent a high-performance convertible. It's red, shiny, and a real head-turner. Just looking at the car increases your heart rate and you can't wait to hit the open road.

As you round a curve enjoying this wonderful moment, you suddenly drive head-on into a fog bank. Out of nowhere the fog encases your car. What is the first thing you do? Most likely, you'll put your foot on the brakes to slow down. Next, you'll put both hands on the wheel and possibly even pull yourself closer to the wheel in the hopes of seeing better. And to help even further, you'll turn down the radio to help you think.

Gone is the carefree and enthusiastic feeling you just had for your trip. Instead, the feeling you are experiencing is adrenaline cascading through your body. You are in survival mode and in this moment you are fighting to survive.

After what seems like minutes, but likely was three-to-five seconds, the fog lifts and you can once again see clearly for miles ahead. The tension that flooded your body in survival mode is gone and the feeling of being safe returns. Slowly the enthusiasm you have for your trip returns and in a few minutes the radio is back on and your foot is on the accelerator.

When we lack a clear and compelling purpose for our leadership, as well as for our teams and organizations, we are driving in fog. There is tension and the enjoyment for our destination evaporates as quickly as the fog obscures our vision. With a clear and compelling purpose, we remove our foot from the brake and squarely hit the accelerator. We accelerate toward our destination with enthusiasm and excitement.

When I ask executives and entrepreneurs what they really want for themselves and for their teams and organizations, nine times out of 10 there is no clear purpose. That leaves employees feeling as though they are driving in fog. Their feet are on the brakes regarding any new ideas and they are inhibited in their capacity to make their customers' lives easier and more rewarding. This is the opposite of what most leaders want and yet it is what the vast majority of leaders are creating.

Every leader has dreams, hopes, and aspirations for his or her professional as well as his or her personal life. In each coaching and consulting engagement I have, the moment a leader's hopes, dreams, and aspirations are clarified, there is a noticeable release of tension and a palpable excitement in the air. It's as if the engine is revving at a higher RPM and the enthusiasm for moving toward the hopes for the future becomes the primary focus.

If you picked up this book in order to create dramatic revenue, performance, and relationship growth, you will not be disappointed. The next section will help you define your purpose and in turn live a more rewarding and enriching life.

Finding Your Purpose in Talent, Love, and Value

Without exception, dramatic performance as well as engagement and satisfaction, both personally and professionally, are closer than you think when you have a clearly articulated purpose. I say "closer than you think" because improvements of almost all types in organizations start with one word: *clarity*. It is used with respect to expectations, results, value, competencies, accountability, and what makes us feel alive and vibrant. Without clarity there is little-to-no likelihood that focus can follow. With clarity and focus come new insights, new strategies, and new behaviors that move individuals and organizations forward in unprecedented ways.

This section is important to you for one reason: All of the other principles of leadership become intellectual constructs as opposed to supporting principles without a clear and compelling purpose. For example, you can go through the motions of the second principle of transformational leadership, the Promises Principle, but it is folly to try and set meaningful and compelling promises if you don't first know what your purpose is. Without question, this section will prove the most pivotal of the whole book.

A few words of caution before we get started: Depending on the mindset you bring to this section, you might have one of two responses to what you read in this section. The first response is one of frustration. You've heard the exhortations from coaches and consultants before, and you've understood for years the linkage between accelerated performance and what a person loves doing, what they're really good at, and what value they bring to their customer, team, or organization.

You have heard the message, but you have also been unable to clarify what each dimension of purpose really means to you. In turn, this section might be seen as laborious and frustrating. Instead of diving into the section with curiosity and courage you turn the page to the next section, telling yourself you will come back to this section later.

The second possible response is one of enthusiasm. You believe that no matter how clear and compelling your purpose, you want to learn a new perspective and possibly alter how you live out your purpose. You welcome the time spent clarifying what's important to you and value growing in your ability to lead with purpose and with passion.

Regardless of your reaction, here's my promise to you for this section: The moment you get crystal clear about your purpose, your level of engagement and enthusiasm will skyrocket. The fog lifts and you'll see miles down the road for you, your team, and your organization, and you'll hit the accelerator. This section will help you get crystal clear if you cultivate two words: *curiosity* and *courage*. You'll need curiosity to pull back the layers of your historical way of viewing the subject of purpose and you'll need courage to think bigger about your leadership than you have in the past.

The Fuel That Propels Greatness

The three dimensions of purpose are: love, talent, and value.

Love is the unbridled enthusiasm you have for your work. When love is present there is a continual striving and leaning into whatever is required to learn, grow, and improve. Without love your talent and value leave you (and others) feeling empty and dissatisfied.

Talent is what you do in highly differentiated ways. Talent is rooted in the skill and expertise you bring to your customers and the relationships that matter most to you. Talent, in many regards, is the price of entry into the world of work today. Lacking talent is a career-limiting move.

Value is the benefit customers or employees derive from interacting with us. Value can be seen as making people's lives easier and better in some meaningful way. Value is not the technical product or service you provide. It is the benefit people receive from using the product or service you provide. Keep in mind that you can have passion for what you do and do it exceptionally well, but if customers or employees see little or no value, your success is in jeopardy.

In order to clarify your purpose, you will want to gain a deeper understanding of how your unique talents, skills, and passions create value for yourself, your customer, and your organization. The following sections will walk you through the process I use with my clients in order to clarify their purpose.

Love

At the heart of excellence lies love. Through your love of something you are motivated to overcome challenges and achieve your biggest hopes, dreams, and aspirations. When you are compelled by what you do, *work* ceases to be a four-letter word. Love is a key component of personal fulfillment and can be found by answering the following four questions:

1. What part of my job do I love doing? Why?
2. What part of my work do I find most rewarding?

3. What is the one idea, hope, dream, or aspiration regarding my work that has grabbed hold of me and won't let go?
4. What aspect of my work, if I were no longer able to do it, would make my work less fulfilling?

To make this real for you, the following is a real-world example from my own leadership.

I am passionate about two things: At work I love converting human potential into accelerated business results and in my personal life I love doing something each day that enables human flourishing. I talk about each one, I read about each one, I learn as much as I can about each one, and I cannot imagine going through the day not doing each one. I am passionate about them.

Talent

What do you do really well? Where do your strengths lie? To answer this question, start by identifying what you do well for your organization. In what ways do you effectively serve your customers and employees? Thinking about talent also provides you with an opportunity to say "I may be talented at something, but I'm not passionate about it." Consider the following questions to help you begin that thinking process.

1. What are my five most important talents and skills?

2. What is my proudest contribution and/or accomplishment? Why?
3. What part of my work do I receive the most compliments about?
4. The five work activities I take great pride in are . . .
5. What part of my job do I plan to master?

I am excellent at listening for the hidden content and context of a person's highest hopes, dreams, and aspirations. This is a gift I was born with and I've done as much as possible to respect it, cultivate it, and improve it. I am also excellent at leadership messaging. I've cultivated this skill because I want leaders to foster human flourishing, and leadership messaging is essential. I am also excellent at priority-setting and executive decision-making, thus providing practical and tactical ideas clients can use immediately to improve the quality of their most important relationships.

Value

Last, but certainly not the least, is value. Clarifying your purpose requires understanding the value your actions create. These outcomes are often more significant than the simple completion of a task.

For example, when you hire someone to mow your lawn, a result is that you have cut grass and a tidy yard. At the same time, there is a more significant relational outcome: You converted time doing a less-important task (doing yard work) to spending time with your family. An important emotional connection is created because you delegated one task and instead invested in your family relationships.

As a precursor to specifically articulating the value you create, answer the following questions to get an idea about your leadership.

1. List as many activities as possible that you do in your role.
2. List a minimum of two results for each activity.
3. Review the activities and results you identified. Which one or ones do you do in distinctive and highly valuable ways?
4. What are your top four most valuable activities?

By answering these questions, what have you learned about your leadership? Can you now answer the following four questions?

1. In my professional life, what are the most valuable contributions I make to my customer, my colleagues or coworkers, and my organization?
2. What aspects of my work are distinctive? What differentiates me from my colleagues who have the same role?

3. What part of my work, if I were to no longer do it, would leave my customer bitterly disappointed?
4. How can I increase the value I bring to my organization?

Each value statement should not mention how you helped your client or customer achieve the result. What is articulated should be increased growth, reduced employee turnover, higher customer satisfaction, and other results. Always keep in mind that people don't care about what tool is used to achieve the result they want. They only care about the value or the outcome they experience.

What Is Your Purpose?

Consider the insights you have had thus far. What ideas are particularly meaningful to you? These insights are the catalyst for your leadership purpose. Now it's time to write your initial purpose statement. This statement should reflect your passion, competencies, and the organizational outcomes for which you want to be known. A template is provided for you, but feel free to write your purpose statement in your own words.

I create *(what you do)* so that *(whoever your customer is)* can achieve *(what)*.

Try It on for Size

Once you have an initial draft of your purpose statement, how does it fit? Take a few minutes to discuss your purpose with someone you trust and respect. If you are bold, talk with a customer and see what his or her reaction is. Does it resonate with you? What, if any, changes will make it a better fit for your leadership?

In the next section we'll talk about how to live out your purpose in meaningful and purposeful ways while building a brand and reputation as someone who creates transformational results.

Be Distinct or Be Extinct

What makes you distinctive? That can be a hard question to answer. We can't see ourselves clearly and oftentimes our mindset pays more attention to what we are not doing well as opposed to what we are doing well. We also have the headwind of working in a world of work in which we are admonished to do more, do it better, do it faster, and do it cheaper. This mantra of performance is never-ending and it leaves us feeling overwhelmed.

The key idea about being distinctive is less about being something to people that you aren't and more about aligning what you are gifted and talented at doing in highly differentiated ways for people who value it.

This is an incredibly simple idea and there is certainly no rocket science here. However, all too often the mindset I find in leaders is that they believe they have to comport themselves to what clients need as opposed to what they can do in beneficial ways. With this belief, satisfaction and performance are tossed out the window.

The jumping-off point for distinction is three-fold. You must have a purpose that is engaging and exciting to you. You have to understand and listen to your customers and employees in ways that provide you with actionable insights. And you have to have a self-confidence that is unshakable. In the last section we addressed the love, talent, and value you provide, and in the next section we will address how to craft a leadership brand and reputation that is highly differentiated. In this section you are going to clarify your most distinctive beliefs and why they are important.

There is a website called *thisibelieve.org*. It is an international organization that engages people in describing the core values that guide their daily lives. You can hear the stories about what people believe on NPR. When I heard this for the first time I was intrigued and thought it an excellent values clarification exercise for my clients. I did the exercise myself and share my answers as a catalyst for you to clarify what you believe. Why? I believe that if you get clear about what you believe, you will focus on making it actionable and real. In total, I have 14 things that I believe.

1. **I believe love makes the world a better place.** Every major faith tradition believes that the world in which we live was created in love and for love and that we have a responsibility to live in alignment with that belief. I believe that *love* is a word far too infrequently used in the corporate world and that by not using it we're shortchanging ourselves, our families, our employees, and our customers.

2. **I believe that generosity is a habit and stems from gratitude.** I believe that people who are ungrateful are incapable of being generous. Generosity can be emotional, spiritual, or financial. Yes, people can write checks out of obligation, but true generosity, giving for the pleasure of giving to another without anticipation of a return, is rooted in a generous mindset. When we are not grateful for what we have we hold on to what we have and lack generosity.

3. **I believe that to those whom much has been given, much is expected.** I have been incredibly blessed in my life, and I believe that in turn it is my role, my responsibility, and yes, my obligation, to share what I've learned with others. I don't expect everyone

to act on what I share, but I do expect them to keep the exchange of success strategies alive.

4. **I believe we need to retire the word *retirement*.** Statistics say that when I reach the age of 65, and if I'm reasonably healthy, I will live to 90. I cannot imagine sitting dormant; many people believe retirement means doing nothing for 25 years. I love what I do, and as long as I am making a contribution to the world, why would I stop?

5. **I believe we need to stop imposing our beliefs and values on others.** We need to jettison the Golden Rule and embrace the Platinum Rule instead. The Golden Rule says that I should treat people as I want to be treated. The Platinum Rule says that I will treat others in ways that they want to be treated as long as they are in accordance with our values and we are not violating them to do so.

6. **I believe we're growing or dying.** If we are not growing, we are dying. If we are not learning something new and thinking differently, we are decaying. Yes, each day I grow or die. Far too many people are content to live life based on outdated mindsets and never challenge what they think, feel, or believe. This is folly par excellence.

7. **I believe in experiencing beauty daily.** Whether in artwork or in a natural landscape,

seeing beauty enriches us and uplifts us. Every day we should look at something beautiful and allow it to stir our soul and enrich our lives. It can be as common as the moon over the water, the sun reflecting off a leaf, or the expression of care or concern that makes someone's day better.

8. **I believe mindset trumps skill set.** I believe there are incredibly talented people who never reach their full potential because their mindset is tainted with issues from the past. Their mindset soils everything that happens to them.

9. **I believe people live in fear.** Fear has become pervasive and is based on past experiences. I believe fear stifles all creativity. In my own life I have had to jettison fear because it was a large part of how I grew up. I think there are far too many people driven by fear.

10. **I believe in assuming positive intent.** There are people we interact with that do not always lead to the best of interactions, but we should assume these people had no ill intent. People are not out to take advantage of us.

11. **I believe in the same starting point, not the same ending point.** I believe society has fostered a victimization and entitlement mindset. There are people who believe they

should have the same outcome in life as someone else. Just because you are able to go into business does not mean you should have the same outcome as everyone else who started the same business. Each of us is entitled to the same starting point, but not the same finishing point.

12. **I believe that being overwhelmed is a choice.** When we lack clear priorities, roles, expectations; when we are not clear on what we can say yes and no to; and when we have not focused on the critical few things that absolutely have to be done, we will feel overwhelmed. Being overwhelmed can be mastered by making one or two choices that allow us to feel empowered and in control.

13. **I believe that life is for savoring.** I believe life can be a feast or a banquet, but the majority of people choose the fast-food drive-through. When we open our eyes to the natural beauty around us and to the interesting people in intriguing locations, we cannot help but marvel at all the teeming life. And yet many people are simply surviving and not savoring life. I think that is a terrible way to live your life.

14. **I believe I can help you live a more rewarding life.** Without question I have a fabulous and very blessed life. I believe that in some

small way, by articulating this list of what I believe, I may help you compile the five, 10, 15, or 20 things you believe. I believe that when you get clear about what you believe, you will hyper-focus on your beliefs and make them become even more of a reality.

Let's return to the question from the beginning of this section. What makes you distinctive? In order to have a clearer perspective of who you are and what makes you distinctive, take time to answer this question: What do I believe? You will see yourself clearly, you will lift the fog covering your work, and you will link what you believe with working in purposeful and highly differentiated ways. Let's now discover whether you are living in accordance with your core beliefs and discover ways to feel invigorated by your work.

What Are You Selling?

There is a quote from a Harley Davidson executive who talked about what Harley Davidson was selling. He said, "What we sell is the ability for a 40-year-old accountant to dress in black leather and ride through small towns and have people be afraid of him." That's a pithy and provocative quote, but it begs the question: What are you selling?

What is the one thing people say you stand for in conversations with customers and employees? Is it excellence in the customer experience? Is it creating a culture in which every employee is engaged in creating the extraordinary? Is it to reduce costs or survive from one layoff to another? Or, are you a leader who is a purveyor of optimism, transformational thinking, and unprecedented growth? Are you selling the idea that in order to have a flourishing business your job as a leader is to help each employee do something daily that allows them and the customer to flourish? Whatever you believe to be important and valuable, are you doing it purposefully and in such a way that people want to buy it?

In this section you'll make the concrete connection between what you believe and what people experience. The two words you'll pay close attention to are *intent* and *impact*. Your intent might be as pure as the driven snow, but your impact could be negative and leave people figuratively running for the hills. As you read this section keep one key point firmly in mind: People never buy what you're selling based on your intent. They buy what you're selling based on how what you do and say impacts them personally.

The Leadership Brand Impact Process

Organizations know about the power of brands. Brands create value, loyalty, and, when compelling and distinctive, they create profound emotional experiences for customers that attract more customers who want the same experience. What is not recognized as much is that a leader's brand can be a catalyst for transformational growth.

Transformational leaders no longer rely solely on their organization's brand to guide their behavior. Transformational leaders develop their own individual brand.

Where do you start? What follows is my Leadership Brand Impact process. There are two key points to start with: First, you have a brand whether you know it or not. Second, the impact your brand has on others is either helping or hurting your performance. The LBI will help you decide whether the impact your brand is having is positive or negative.

The process I'll outline requires courage. It's not for the faint of heart. You will ask people who are important to you about your impact and see clearly, maybe for the first time, the impact you have on people. Some of what you'll hear will be incredibly uplifting and inspirational. Other aspects will leave you uncomfortable and/ or embarrassed. But rest assured, you cannot change anything unless you see it clearly. The LBI will help you with that.

Step 1

Clarify the brand impact you intended. Take 10 minutes to write down the impact you want to have on the people who matter most to you. The starting point for understanding the impact your brand has on others involves writing four words or phrases that you believe best describe your leadership. Don't overthink this; simply capture what you see as the essence of your leadership.

For example, you may use words such as inspiring, collaborative, thoughtful, and pragmatic.

Step 2

Clarify the brand impact people experience. This step starts by creating a list of eight to 10 people who you trust and respect. They can be colleagues, managers, coworkers, direct reports, former employees, and friends. Your list should consist of people whose opinions you value.

Call or speak in person with those on your list and let them know you are involved in a leadership activity that requires candid feedback. As someone you respect, his or her assistance in seeing the impact of your leadership from an outsider's perspective is essential.

Specifically, ask them to provide you with four words or phrases they believe best describe the impact your leadership has on them and others. It might be a one-word descriptor such *innovative* or *inspiring*. It can also include phrases such as *can-do attitude*.

Step 3

This step reviews the 32 to 40 words that represent what others see as your Leadership Brand Impact. Review your words and compile a list of themes or patterns. Similar words or synonyms should be distilled into a one-word descriptor that best represents what you believe is the tone and/or feel of the words.

The overarching objective in this step is to clarify your Leadership Brand Impact from other perspectives and distill it into the fewest words possible. This will allow you to study your two lists and look for gaps between what you intended and what people experienced. Is there a gap between your intended brand impact and the brand impact listed by your observers? While looking at your list, ask yourself the following questions:

1. Is my intent aligned with my impact?
2. Am I being seen in ways consistent with my purpose?
3. Are my brand impact descriptors (both my own and from my observers) distinctive or simply the price of entry for being in my role?
4. What is the upside and downside to my leadership brand/reputation?
5. Am I excited about the words used to describe me, or am I neutral?

No doubt, there are words on your lists that are aligned with what you intended and others that are not. Transformational leaders grow up and take responsibility for the impact they have on others.

Step 4

This step will help you clarify the behaviors you'll adopt to create the brand impact you want. It asks three simple yet important questions:

1. What is the impact I want to be known for?
2. If I want to be known for XYZ, what traits, characteristics, behaviors, and or values will I embody in order to create my desired impact?
3. What will become essential and/or non-negotiable to me?

This last step is less about logic and more about what's probable; it is rooted in articulating your highest hopes, dreams, and aspirations for the impact your leadership has. This step converts the insights you've gleaned from the LBI and asks you to become behaviorally explicit about what you will implement based on your insights. This step is essential. If you gloss over this step the LBI will become an intellectually interesting exercise but won't lead to anything noteworthy or transformational.

Showing up is where the rubber meets the road. Showing up requires focusing daily on how you communicate, hold meetings, delegate, hold people accountable, talk with customers, and deal with adversity and uncertainty, and calibrating whether or not your impact leads people to buy what you're selling.

Step 5

In this step, leaders go to all of the people who provided feedback, as well as their key constituents, and share the impact they want to have. They show up in a real and transparent way about what they learned about their leadership, what insights they've gleaned about their impact, and what they will do differently.

They now give people permission to tell them when what they are doing is not aligned with what they said. They don't just give people permission, they continually and frequently ask for advice from people about how they can live out the leadership brand in powerful, purposeful, and compelling ways.

The clients who have used the LBI successfully report that this process was transformational for them. They felt as though the Scottish poet Robert Burns was right when he said, in effect, that seeing ourselves as others see us is essential. They also said they are 60 percent more effective by having gone through this process. I hope that is the case for you as well. In the next section you integrate everything you've learned and jump into creating your ideal day.

Your Ideal Day Is Waiting

Can every day be an ideal day? No, it can't. Will the choices we make increase the possibility that the number of days we experience as an ideal day increase? Yes, absolutely.

Here's my bold admonition: Living an ideal day is a choice. There's no way around the fact that we have a choice as to how we choose to plan and live our days. In his book *Man's Search for Meaning*, psychologist Viktor Frankl recounted how, in the face of the unfathomable horror, deprivation, and cruelty of a German concentration camp, he could choose his experience. He didn't simply put on rose-colored glasses and think happy thoughts. He chose to accept his circumstances and focused on his hopes for what he would experience and accomplish after his release.

Viktor Frankl didn't delegate his choices for his daily experiences either. He chose his experiences and worked tirelessly in the concentration camp to share his choice with fellow prisoners. He unquestioningly posited that we all have a choice as to how we experience and live our day.

Of course there are days when you will walk into the office knowing you will terminate an employee with two children in college and a new home. No one will disagree that situations such as those are hard and challenging. But far too often leaders see only the negative. They view work as a four-letter word and see their days as filled with land mines, a relentless need to do more, do it faster, and do it cheaper, and an onslaught of political, manipulative, or lazy people who make their day frustrating and challenging.

Viewing your day this way has you arriving home only to greet your family or friends exhausted, overwhelmed, and incapable of a meaningful connection. This type of day has you checked out emotionally at home because you've used up all of your emotional energy simply surviving the day. Which day are you choosing? Are you choosing an ideal day of *your* making or a day simply responding to the exigencies of the day?

You're Closer Than You Think

The good news is that your ideal is much closer than you think. It's a simple shift in perspective or belief. Eight years ago my wife grew exasperated sleeping next to me. My snoring was waking her in the middle of the night even though she was wearing ear plugs. I scheduled a sleep study and learned I had a mild case of sleep apnea. A CPAP machine allowed me to wake in the morning without the feeling of having gone 15 rounds with a heavyweight boxer.

My sleep quality increased, but my sleep quantity didn't. I was waking at 2:30 a.m. and staying awake for 45 minutes to an hour. When asleep, I had high-quality sleep, but I wasn't sleeping long enough.

I worked with a sleep coach (yes, there are such people) and learned that an increase in sleep quantity was closer than I thought. The perspective I brought to my sleep was that going to bed earlier was the prescription I needed. The opposite was the case for me. I needed to go to bed 45 minutes later; by doing so I would sleep without interruption throughout the night. It was counterintuitive.

I learned two important lessons: The first is that coaches are the fastest way to increased performance and the best way to make performance sustainable. The second lesson is that we are most often closer to our ideal than we can see. When we have a shift in perspective it changes the way we act and respond. By changing the way we act and respond, we change the results we get. Living our ideal day is that simple and shouldn't be made any more complicated.

Where Do You Start?

In the previous sections you identified what you love doing, what you're good at, and what value you bring to your team and organization. You've articulated what you believe and what makes you distinctive in the eyes of your most important relationships, and you've seen your leadership impact through the eyes of the people who are important to you. With this backdrop, there are three things you need to do in order to live your ideal day. You must reframe your past, reclaim your future, and recalibrate your present.

Reframe Your Past

You have to be able to look at the negative events in your past and say, "It may not have been ideal, but here's how I'm going to view these events and what I've learned." In choosing to focus on what is positive you become highly resilient. That shapes your reactions and behaviors in positive ways. This can be hard at times, but reframing negative experiences into positive ones is incredibly powerful and within your control. What one, two, or three experiences do you want to reframe? I chose to reframe the repossessing of our furniture from the loss of personal possession to the gaining of tenacity, discipline, and perseverance.

Reclaim Your Future

In order to have high hopes for your ideal day there must be dreams, aspirations, or big ideas that have grabbed hold of you and that you have said yes to. Big dreams or aspirations leave us acting like a gambler who goes all in. In that moment, the conversation is "Under no circumstances will I take no for an answer on this type of personal and professional life. This is the life I am claiming." When you live your leadership purpose there is no way out and there is no backdoor. When you say, "I will accomplish this," you have reclaimed the idealized day you have in mind.

Recalibrate Your Present

Recalibrating your present requires discerning what things you should not do again and what you absolutely should do again. This strategy requires recalibrating what worked and what didn't work throughout the course of the last year. What was something that accelerated your performance and your sense of satisfaction? What created hope for you, and what created anxiety? Identify the areas of your present that will get in your way and do whatever you can to reduce them or eliminate them. Find those things that are going to help you create growth and double down on them.

If you reframe your past, reclaim your future, and recalibrate your present you can live your ideal day. But be forewarned: The most revolutionary act you can ever take is to claim your ideal day and to move toward it with faith, confidence, and a deep sense of resolve. When you articulate your ideal day it's essential that you share it with someone you trust and respect. When you share your ideal day and that you are pursuing it, it becomes real and tangible. It doesn't mean every day will be ideal, but it does mean the number of ideal days you have will increase appreciably.

The following chapters support all of the work you've done so far. In the next chapter specifically, you apply what you've learned in ways that are professionally rewarding as well as exciting in their ability to dramatically increase the level of growth you want in revenue, performance, and the quality of your personal and professional relationships.

2

The Promises Principle

The Difference Between Promises, Commitments, and Vows

Four years ago, my wife Alyson found a great house in a quiet beach community one block off Puget Sound. She was convinced that the home, which had not been updated since it was built in 1957, would be a fabulous blank canvas from which we could create our northwest contemporary oasis overlooking Puget Sound. I didn't see it. I saw a house with a chopped-up floor plan, old carpet, no office, and a rooster next door that would drive me bonkers.

But Alyson took me on three tours and created a mental picture that I started to see. She won me over when we walked into the downstairs area and she stood me in front of a fireplace. She turned me around to look out a 6-foot by 10-foot window that faced the water. She said, "This is the world headquarters of Claris Consulting. This space will be your office. I promise you this will be the space that inspires you and creates the mindset for you to do your best work."

I believed her and signed the power of attorney for her to purchase the house while I was on a three-week business trip.

What Is a Promise?

A promise is an abiding commitment, an assurance to others that we will or will not do something. Alyson promised me the office of my dreams and she did everything she could to make it happen, including delaying other improvements so that I could have it. By delaying the kitchen remodel, she communicated clearly that her promises were not simply words used to sucker me in to buying the house. No, she meant it, even if it required delaying improvements to the area of the house she dreamed of having.

There are five powerful lessons about promises I learned from Alyson.

1. Promises without a higher purpose or objective have little-to-no positive impact.
2. Promises are voluntary and never forced.
3. Promises require saying no as much as saying yes.
4. Promises to people we care about carry tremendous weight.
5. Promises are about credibility and trust.

The Purpose of Promises

Alyson clearly saw what I couldn't see and knew that, although I couldn't see right away what the house would look like, in time I'd catch up to her. She was steadfast in creating the vision we had for our house. She focused on having a home with water and mountain views, lots of natural light, clean and contemporary space, room for entertaining, and an office for me. Her decisions were geared to making our vision real. Her promise for my office had a powerful impact on me because I knew she wanted the same thing for me professionally.

Promises are voluntary and not ever forced. Promises must be voluntary. When promises are made solely to placate someone or to get a foot in the door only to turn the tables and renegotiate the outcome, the promises come across as hollow and manipulative. Alyson voluntarily made promises about the schedule of our home remodel without coercion and in turn communicated volumes about what mattered most: having the home of our dreams in a way that worked for both of us.

Promises also require saying no. With our home we knew the budgeting advice we got was accurate. Get three bids, add them together, and that's how much the remodel will cost. We knew we would have to say no to certain things. For example, the bathrooms would come last. From a leadership perspective, Alyson led the charge with our contractor and repeatedly had to say no to ideas for improvements. With a budget of one million dollars we could have said yes to more ideas, but we didn't have a budget of that size, so saying no became essential. The same holds true with making promises. If you say yes to a promise, what must you say no to in order to fulfill your promise?

When we make promises to people we care about, they carry tremendous weight. Promises are not going to be made to a telemarketer who calls at 8 p.m. on a Wednesday evening. If a promise *is* made, it is made with the intent of jettisoning the call as soon as possible. A promise made to a child, a spouse, or a boss is a totally different situation. When we make promises to people who are important to us, the promise takes on a higher level of importance as well as a higher level of commitment to accomplishing it.

Credibility and trust are the components of promises. Without exception, kept promises do more for a leader's credibility and trustworthiness with employees and customers than any leadership development initiative. Actually, the one cardinal rule to be the type of leader people are willing to follow is incredibly simple: Do what you say you will do. That's what Alyson did in a high-stakes home remodel. When each budget estimate by our contractor was missed she did what she always said she would do and never wavered. In this critical environment where money was being hemorrhaged I could always trust her to know what to do.

Why should you care about the promises you make? You should care because your employees and customers have heard leaders make promises before and not fulfill them. They are jaded, disengaged, and distrusting of leaders to the point that they are simply tolerating most leaders. When leaders tell people what they want to hear and then do something else they create a credibility gap that leaves employees disbelieving the message simply because they disbelieve the messenger.

The promises we make to ourselves can inspire trustworthiness; yet how easily are these promises broken? Sometimes it may seem that our work and home lives are weighed down by everything that appears to require our attention. Consequently, we struggle to keep our promises to others and ourselves. Because we have not planned to honor our promises, they have little chance of being fulfilled. In the Promise Principle, you'll examine how kept promises enhance your leadership and further your purpose.

Promise Evaluation

Consider the discrete types of promises you make in your work and home life. Promise types may include meeting deadlines, delivering work on budget, following through on a commitment to a colleague, choosing to act in ways that further your purpose, and so on. Make a list of eight to 12 promises you typically make. Once you have your list, rank how you uphold these promises on a 5-point scale (1 = easily broken to 5 = always honored).

Answer the following questions and then look at your list and rankings.

1. What types of promises do you follow through on?
2. In what situations is it more difficult to keep your promises?
3. What are the relational outcomes of these choices?
4. How do these promises relate to your purpose?

In order for you to fully live out your purpose, what two or three promises are necessary that you make to *yourself*? What are the important promises you want from yourself that are in alignment with your purpose?

In order for you to fully live out your purpose, what two or three promises are necessary that you make to your employees, customers, boss, board, and your family and friends? What are the important promises you want to make that are in alignment with your purpose and that foster increased credibility and trust?

Before you move to the section on why the absence of promises creates apprehension, ambiguity, and uncertainty, stop and list your non-negotiable promises. These are the promises you will make to the people that matter most to you. If those people really matter, you will not keep your promises solely in your head. You'll put a pen to paper and make your promises concrete and tangible.

Why Apprehension, Ambiguity, and Uncertainty Flourish Without Promises

What is the root of apprehension, ambiguity, and uncertainty? At the center of each word is *fear*. If I am apprehensive, I am afraid of the unknown. When ambiguity is present I am unsure of what might happen. With uncertainty, I might be afraid about what I should do next. I don't want to fail or lose something important, so I hold back.

In each case, smart, talented, and well-meaning employees stand on the sidelines rather than running on to the field of play yelling "put me in the game." This is a recipe for underperformance.

Far too many of us live in fear when it comes to our business lives. For some of us, it's financial fear. For others, it's emotional. No matter the source or type, fear has a debilitating effect on personal and professional growth over extended periods of time. Fear can be a catalyst for action, but inspired performance and accelerated progress can never be realized in the shadow of a fearful mindset.

Some people say that fear can be a positive element in our lives. That may be true when it comes to having a healthy dose of caution against overtly risky behavior, but in the business world, letting fear take control is paramount to self-sabotage. When we're fearful, we play not to lose instead of playing to win.

I was told recently that the statement "Do not be afraid" (or a similar admonition) appears 365 times in the Bible. That's once for every day of the year. Consider for a moment what would happen if you told yourself that no one was out to get you, and that you wouldn't be pelted with tomatoes while locked in stockades.

Instead, what if you promised yourself and your employees to direct all of your emotional and intellectual horsepower into taking proactive approaches to challenges? What would happen to your performance if you promised to create powerful proactive solutions to problems at work and at home while shedding the anxiety of a fearful mindset? I believe it would be a freeing and empowering promise to make.

Let's be clear about one key point: In the business world, performance decreases as fear increases. If performance is decreasing and your markets are maintaining or increasing, I guarantee you that some sort of fear is behind it. The fear might take the form of anxiety about a new job or responsibility. It could also be financial fear of budget cuts or lack of resources. Either way, this mindset contributes to a loss of progress in the organization and requires new promises to correct it.

The best way to fight fear is to identify what causes it. If you can determine the cause of fear, you can redirect it and make it less frightening for you and your team. Throughout my extensive work with executives and entrepreneurs as a coach and mentor, I have discovered seven types of fear that are most common. Take a moment to consider each one and identify the ones that are challenging to you.

1. Fear of Accountability

The fear of accountability is two-fold. For leaders, there is a fear that by holding someone accountable they might get upset or challenge your perspective. In one organization I worked with, the senior executive was afraid of holding people accountable due to her behavior style. She was direct, to the point, and a bottom-line leader. Her direct reports were relationship-focused, harmony-driven, and conflict-adverse. This leader was afraid that her way of leading would be offensive and her employees felt that her approach to seeking accountability would be abrasive and hurtful. In turn, the promise on the table was that clear expectations, increased accountability regarding metrics, and best-of-class processes would be addressed only if it was comfortable. If anyone felt uncomfortable the conversation ended.

2. Fear of Making Mistakes

The fear of making mistakes can be real in many organizations. In one strategic planning session, I heard the senior vice president of operations wax poetically about risk-taking and improved performance, only to instill fear and trepidation by saying with stern conviction, "Of course, your risk-taking must be successful." His only option was to succeed and failure was tantamount to treason. It's no surprise the majority of employees chose to not risk the uncertainty of, well, risk-taking. The unspoken but powerful promise from this executive was *succeed or you'll be gone.*

3. Fear of Leaving a Job That Sucks the Energy Out of You

The 50-year-old (and older) executives with whom I speak are afraid of leaving their jobs due to age discrimination. This fear is multiplied if you are female. Are some organizations biased toward younger employees? Yes. Is discrimination real? Yes. However, the realities can be overblown. This fear doesn't actively consider the value created by an executive or the goodwill and brand developed through years of doing noteworthy work.

What I've found in this particular situation is the root fear of not being confident in oneself to find the ideal day and life that brings us alive. Without a promise to ourselves about creating and cultivating our ideal day, we promise ourselves to remain in jobs and organizations that suck the energy out of us rather than help us come alive.

4. Fear of Not Being Seen As Smart and Successful

At its core, this fear is rooted in self-doubt. It is the quintessential imposter syndrome in which employees and leaders see themselves as "lucky to have a job" as opposed to "so talented that the company is fortunate to have them." I worked with one leader who had five degrees from Ivy League schools, and whose IQ was higher than

99 percent of not only the general population but also of his colleagues. In talking with him I realized that the primary reason he had five degrees was to convince himself he was smart and successful. This insecurity promised one thing to his colleagues: Whenever he was engaged in discussion about issues pertaining to work he would do everything imaginable to be seen as the smartest person in the room. His fear squelched innovation, collaboration, and increased performance.

5. Fear of Upsetting Your Boss or Senior Leaders

The fear of upsetting your boss or senior leaders is most commonly associated with bringing bad news. This fear can be rooted in a person's insecurity, or it can be rooted in a boss's intolerance for bad news. Some bosses are afraid of bad news so they put on Kevlar body armor to repel all bad news. When employees are afraid of either experiencing the wrath of an unhappy boss or of wasting their time or energy, they promise themselves to avoid the situation and allow someone else to be the bearer of bad news. This strategy never works well.

6. Fear of Turning Away From Current Success to Have Even Greater Success

There are teams and leaders who view success as mere luck. They think they were in the right place at the right time and their success cannot be replicated. This perspective shows up whenever new ideas are presented but then dismissed with the proverbial "that's not the way we've done things in the past." Leaders can learn a lot from the past, but the real courageous act is to leave the confines of the known, predictable, and certain, and challenge ourselves to think and act differently. The promise of maintaining the status quo is misguided unless the status quo involves continual experimentation and innovation.

7. Fear of Investing in Oneself

Without question the fastest and most sustainable way to grow is to work with a coach or mentor. For seven years I've worked with a mentor by the name of Alan Weiss. He is the rock star of consulting and has written 64 books on solo consulting. Without reservation, my return on investment for working with Alan is tenfold. And yet, too many leaders are reticent to work with a coach or mentor because they are afraid to invest in themselves. This is foolhardy. The greatest return on investment a leader can make is to promise himself, as well as the employees, that personal and professional growth is imperative, and that he will be a role model for others by working with a coach or mentor. When leaders do so they send a clear message that growth is not an intellectual idea. It is a promise that is non-negotiable.

Which fear most hinders your performance? Which fear most hinders employee performance? If none of these fears are issues, what fear do you wrestle with the most? This section seeks to reduce employees' uncertainty and apprehension with an assurance of what they can expect and rely on from their leaders. As a transformational leader, you have the opportunity to help your employees feel more secure in their work and, in turn, to do higher-quality and more valuable work.

Take a few minutes to brainstorm a list of the ways or topics around which employees feel uncertainty, apprehension, or ambiguity at work. Then, brainstorm a list of three promises you can make to mitigate some of these fears. Your ideas are the jumping-off point for our next section, which discusses how promises influence people's behavior.

Promises as a Tool to Influence Behavior

In this section you will look at the six ways a promise influences behavior and clarify how the promises you are making or will make are influencing your most important relationships. Promises influence people's behavior in one of two ways: A promise kept builds trust, respect, and credibility. A promise broken does the opposite. Broken promises not only have an impact on the task and technical aspects of work, but they also have a much greater negative impact on the relational aspects of leadership.

How would you react to a colleague breaking a promise she made to you? It would likely depend on the size of the promise made or its importance to you. What is the relational impact on broken promises? If you lost sleep over your colleagues hindering you from delivering a project on time the impact would be substantial. How important is the frequency of broken promises with your colleague? A one-time event is viewed differently than a continual stream of broken promises. What advice do you give to others when a promise is broken? In order for promises to have a positive influence on other people there are three must-have aspects of a promise that have to be considered.

1. Promises Must Create Alignment Around a Clear Future State

Promises communicate in clear and compelling language the destination each party is headed. There are no general ideas or themes with a promise, but rather specifics. An issue might be to seek out and retain a new supplier. The process of doing so might take three weeks, but as long as there are promises made for having a new supplier option, you can have a clear line of sight for increasing production capacity, increasing on-time deliveries, and sleeping better. The clear future state helps you reduce your anxiety, which increases your effectiveness and your performance as the production manager.

Promises also create alignment. Cars with wheels out of alignment waste energy and burn through tires. When the wheels are aligned the inefficiency of the misalignment is removed and the longevity of the tires increases appreciably. It's the same with promises. The moment there is clarity as to what both parties want, the energy wasted with misaligned expectations, results, and alternatives is eliminated.

2. Promises Must Clarify Results and Expectations

Embedded in each promise is also a clarification of results and expectations. For example, when a leader promises to accomplish a key result and the expectations surrounding the result, they are also by default defining the results and expectations of others directly or indirectly impacted by the promise. Without question, in our do more, do it faster, and do it better and cheaper world of work, clarifying in crystal-clear terms the desired results and expectations leaves direct reports feeling increased confidence and a renewed sense of optimism.

3. Promises Must Have Clear Communication

There is a key premise with promises. Whenever we communicate expectations and results via our promises, we must accept 100 percent responsibility for the impact our words have on the other person. Gone are the days when a leader can indemnify themselves with the "That's not what I meant" excuse. Clear communication, especially around results and expectations, requires leaders to understand the communication preferences of the people they are communicating with and communicate in ways that work best for them, not in ways that work best for the leaders.

The accompanying premise is that people who have been promised something will only extend flexibility and understanding when the other person does not make excuses for not fulfilling their promise. This is essential for heightened credibility and trustworthiness, for example, what is described in the following response: "I blew this. I got distracted by a last-minute request by my boss. I'm not using that as an excuse, but rather providing some context as to what got in my way. If I do it by 3 p.m. on Friday will that work?"

There is one last piece about clear communication that is important. When trust and respect are in place, most people will assume positive intent and act accordingly. A leader's primary job is to exemplify trustworthiness and respectfulness. When they do, their credibility increases.

• • •

No doubt you have made promises to strategic priorities you need to fulfill. You cannot be an effective leader without doing so. However, what is often missing are compelling and courageous promises about the impact your leadership will have on others. Building on what you articulated in the "What Are You Selling?" and "Your Ideal Day Is Waiting" sections of the Purpose Principle, what promises will you make to the people who matter most to you?

There are five promises that transformational leaders make. They are:

1. Promises to yourself.
2. Promises to your employees.
3. Promises to your customers.
4. Promises to your boss and senior leaders.
5. Promises to your family and friends.

Before moving on to the section on the peril of promises made without a purpose, draft one to three promises for each of the five areas listed. Here are a few examples from my work as an advisor to use as a catalyst for your thinking.

Promises to yourself: I promise that regardless of the demands I'll face at work, I will exercise Monday, Wednesday, and Friday at 6 a.m. for 60 minutes. I will also eat healthfully three times a week by myself and use that time to recharge, refocus, and renew my enthusiasm for my work.

Promises to your employees: I promise that I will lead the charge with the team to focus equally on what we as a team are doing well and what we need to improve. This will not be rote or simply a to-do item on my list, but rather a promise to keep the team focused on the positive work they're accomplishing.

Promises to your customers: I promise as my primary goal to make your lives easier. I will ask for your feedback and your advice as to how we're doing and I promise to take action on your advice. I will tell you what I heard, what I can do differently, and when you can expect to see it.

Promises to your boss and senior leaders: I promise to never bring you problems without solutions unless I'm at a loss for what to do. I also promise to respectfully and purposefully disagree with you in private and support you in public.

Promises to your family and friends: I promise to have dinner with you twice a week at 6:30 p.m. and to have my phone off while we are eating dinner. You are important to me and, although my time is constrained, I promise to make the time we have together the highest quality possible.

Each of the five areas needs to be addressed. Promises to yourself without promises to others is self-absorbed and communicates that you are the most important person in the relationship. Promises to others without corresponding promises to oneself leads to victimization and martyrdom. What promises will you make and to whom?

Priorities Without Purpose Are a Catalyst for Lower Performance

Before we dive into setting priorities, I want to commend you for doing the heavy lifting of clarifying your purpose and declaring your promises. When you work through the exercises of the Purpose Principle, you come to the Promises Principle with high hopes of having your purpose become real. Make no mistake, this is a substantial piece of leadership development that while challenging, will provide you with 10 significant advantages. When viewed together these advantages become the catalyst for you accomplishing transformational work and creating a mindset of passion, innovation, and growth.

1. Clarity

The number-one benefit to having a defined and compelling purpose is that you know what's important to you and why it's important. This is not a small issue. Without question, the most successful leaders I've worked with have clarity around the compelling reason for doing what they do. They have found their one big idea and work tirelessly to accomplish it. This affords them a clear line of sight into where they are heading and the focus to make it a reality.

2. Control

With your purpose you'll have greater control. Not over what happens to you, but over the choices you make in response to what happens as well as to the type of professional life you want to experience. When leaders work through articulating what they love, what their talents are, and what value they create, they are undertaking the most significant aspect of leadership. With a compelling purpose, you feel a heightened sense of control because your professional life is no longer determined by the desires and directives of senior leaders inside your organization. You are in the driver's seat of your profes-sional life and no longer in the backseat hoping to arrive at a worthwhile destination.

3. Consistency

In order to be consistent, leaders have to know what they want to do and when it's important to do so. In the first sections of this book you have been given the opportunity to articulate what you believe is important to you and what you are not willing to leave unfinished. Inconsistency comes if—and this is a big *if*—you don't believe fully in your purpose and any extenuating prom-ises. Claiming your purpose places a flag in the ground that says, "Thus far and no farther." You are jettisoning the days of missteps and false starts and are intentionally committing to do what you say you will do. You will lead more consistently with a clear articulation of what you believe in and what you stand for.

4. Commitment

There is a world of difference between commitment and compliance. Compliance is rooted in doing something if you want to and when you get around to doing it. When asked to finish a report a colleague might say, "Well, yes, we should do that. But as you know I've got vaca-tion coming up and right after we return the kids are back in school, and I'm teaching a new class at church."

Commitment, on the other hand, sounds very different. It sounds like: "Yes, the report is important and I'll have it to you by Friday next week at noon." When you write your leadership purpose you are in many ways writing your declaration of leadership independence. It is something you, like the founding fathers of America, will act on decisively. Your purpose is a commitment to living a purposeful life as opposed to an accidental life.

5. Credibility

People pay attention to what you say and what you do. Any gap between what you say and what you do leads people to question your intentions, sincerity, and credibility. Transformational leaders recognize that what they say matters and they strive to create clear promises about what can be expected of them—not solely for their own benefit, but for everyone involved. When they act consistently, credibility increases, and leadership effectiveness rises as does organizational performance.

6. Confidence

It is counterintuitive, but your confidence as a leader increases appreciably not when you see the benefits of your purpose being realized, but when you believe in your purpose to the point at which you can say without hesitation, "This is what I want and I'm going to achieve it." You've heard the often-repeated bromide, "I'll believe it when I see it." Transformational leaders don't think that way. They adopt the perspective of "I'll see it when I believe it." This is not blind naiveté on a leader's part. Yes, they recognize that the sixth principle of transformational leadership, the Perseverance Principle, is essential for transformational results. But they also know with certainty that if their mindsets and the mindsets of those around them are hesitant and uncertain, the likelihood of accomplishing transformational results is considerably lower. In turn, their confidence is not in the absoluteness of accomplishment, but in the absoluteness of having a compelling purpose as well as a replicable process for achieving transformational results.

7. Community

A compelling leadership purpose attracts likeminded leaders, colleagues, and stakeholders. With all of the other advantages listed here, leaders who are leading on purpose share what is important to them and become a magnet for others who aspire to create the same type of experience for themselves as well as for others. Their behavior and beliefs call to other leaders who have similar hopes, dreams, and aspirations, and together they create a community rooted in shared aspirations. Communities of like-minded collaborators become a place of inspiration, aspiration, and accelerated growth for everyone involved.

8. Candor

For many leaders the level of candor they display after clarifying their purpose goes up appreciably. With a clear purpose comes the clarity, commitment, and confidence to speak the truth as to what the leader wants, how she will act to achieve it, and where she as a leader is hitting the mark and where it is being missed. Purpose becomes the catalyst for less hedging in conversations because when transformational leaders believe strongly in their purpose, they are compelled to say and do something daily to achieve it.

9. Collaboration

In order for leaders to have a clear purpose they'll have had to get clear about what they love doing and what talents and skills they have that they use in highly differentiated ways. They know the value they provide and no longer feel a high need to prove themselves to others. Knowing this allows the leaders to be more comfortable in their own leaderships and in turn invites people to share what they love and are good at to the situation or project. The level of interpersonal competition goes down and the level of innovation and growth increases. Without question, transformational leaders know that in many situations two heads are better than one. When you work through the Projects Principle and the Persuasion

Principle you learn how to choose which heads you want working on your projects.

10. Courage

The word *courage* comes from the French word *cœur*, which means "heart." The first question you were asked in the process of articulating your purpose was, "What do you love doing?"; in essence, what is at the heart of your work and what are you not willing to leave undone? Your answer is at the heart of your leadership. And yet, courage doesn't mean that fear is banished and you'll never have to be courageous. On the contrary, the most courageous act you'll have on a daily basis is whether to live out your purpose or allow the disruptions and exigencies of your work life to dictate your behavior. With a clear and compelling purpose, the reserves of courage you'll find in your leadership will amaze you. You'll think bigger and set more aggressive goals and love the shift of your mindset on yourself as well as on others.

● ● ●

You undoubtedly have experienced some of these advantages and not others. The vast majority of the leaders I work with want these advantages. Who wouldn't? And yet, what is clearly within their reach remains elusive for one reason and one reason only: They have not taken the time to think through what it is they love doing, what they can do in highly differentiated ways, and how they make people's lives easier.

The jumping-off point for achieving transformational results is the Purpose Principle, and setting priorities for your leadership without a clear and compelling purpose is a recipe for maximum frustration and lower performance. Before turning the page and setting your priorities, do a gut check and ask yourself the following question: Is my purpose important enough that I'm willing to make non-negotiable promises to my key stakeholders as well as change my calendar with new and compelling priorities? If the answer is yes, you'll love the next section. If your answer is no, review the Purpose Principle and find one idea that has grabbed hold of you and won't let go. Isolating your one idea, dream, hope, or aspiration becomes one of the most exciting, liberating, and transformational events you will experience as a leader.

When Everything Is a Priority, Nothing Is a Priority

What is a priority? The word *priority* comes from the Anglo-Norman French word *priorie*, which means "elder or superior of a religious order." A priory is a small monastery or nunnery governed by a prior or a prioress. In today's world, a priority is something governed by a higher order. In this section I'll make the case that your highest priorities are best derived from your purpose and promises. Doing this purposefully as opposed to accidentally is the purpose of this section.

As someone who struggled with priority-setting, I can say firsthand that setting priorities without a clear idea of my purpose or the promises I made was a fool's errand. I would set priorities based on the shiny object in front of me while being enamored with the newness of the idea and its inherent possibilities. I believed all of my priorities could or should be implemented immediately but lacked the ability to discern the relative importance each one held and in turn set meaningful and clear priorities.

Unless, of course, it had to do with money. For a large part of my business life the most important priority I had was to make money, be successful, and progress in my career. That was my priority. And with that as a priority I placed at the head of the line business transactions that were driven by financial reward. Although financial reward is not a bad thing, I took it to an extreme. My mindset was rooted in a poverty mindset and led me to look for ways to advance my financial well-being as fast as possible. That meant my financial well-being was a priority over the well-being of others, my health, and my personal relationships. I'm not proud to say that, but I had a disordered attachment to money.

Your mindset too shapes your priorities. Imagine not eating for three days. We'll agree that food will become a priority for you and exercise and cardiovascular endurance become less of a priority. If you have been out of work for two years and have pulled your children out of college because of a lack of resources it goes without saying that having a paycheck is a priority for you and that loving the job that you do would become a secondary priority.

The vast majority of my clients do not have locating their next meal or finding a paycheck as a priority. Their number-one priority is accomplishing their to-do list. They have become, as I once heard someone refer to our work lives, "A human doing as opposed to a human being." They've become so engrossed in checking off items on their to-do list that they've become blind to asking if they have the right priorities on their list.

The good news is that increased effort isn't the answer to better priority-setting. What *is* required is greater hindsight, clearer foresight, and a ruthless determination to say yes to taking one action every day that is aligned with your purpose and your promises. Most leaders are saying yes to an ever-expanding list of priorities—priorities they will likely never be able to accomplish because of a finite amount of time and resources.

Yes, increased effort is essential in some circumstances, but what leaders need more is an increased amount of courage and confidence to have clear rules for what they will say yes to and what they will say no to. Without this courage and confidence leaders will continually feel as though they are falling behind. Here are two quick and easy processes for seeing your priority-setting in action.

Greater Hindsight

To see clearly what priorities you've set, review your calendar for the last four weeks and answer the following two questions:

1. With clarity as to what my purpose is, can I say with confidence that if someone were to review my calendar they would know what's important to me and what I care about? If so, why? If not, what would they think my priorities were?
2. What promises have I valued or ignored based upon how and where I am spending my time?

Clearer Foresight

The following is a quick gut checklist of five questions that address your priority-setting skills.

1. **How many priorities do you have?** Do you have more than five priorities? If you do, you have too many—especially if they are key, mission-critical priorities.
2. **What is a priority to you?** What is the one thing you wake up thinking about and go to bed worrying about? Whatever is repeatedly on your mind is a priority for you. Is it achievement, a promotion, a raise, dealing with the union or dealing with management, or increasing revenue or profit? Whatever is

always on your mind is being made a priority for you.

3. **Are your customers a priority?** If your customers were asked whether they thought they were a high priority for you and your organization, would you hear a resounding yes? Not a wishy-washy yes, but a resounding yes. If yes, why is that and what priorities must you keep having, stop having, or start having in order to maintain this success? If no, what needs to be a priority to correct this?

4. **Are your employees a priority?** If your employees were asked if they are a high priority of yours would you hear a resounding yes? Again, not a wishy-washy yes, but a resounding yes. If yes, why is that and what priorities must you keep having, stop having, or start having in order to maintain this success? If no, what needs to be a priority to correct this?

5. **Is there alignment between your purpose, promises, and priorities?** What are your boss's/organization's highest priorities for you? Are they aligned with your leadership purpose and promises?

The reality is that leadership effectiveness is accelerated when a ruthless choice is made about what priorities to set. This book sets out to show you how to set priorities based on your purpose and promises and how to live them out on a daily basis. There are two forces that have to be understood in the case of effective priority-setting, however.

The first is the opposing forces that hinder you from fulfilling your promises and purpose, and the second is the promoting forces. The promoting forces are the ones that help you fulfill your promises and purpose. We'll look at both with one caveat: Setting clear priorities does not require you to overthink the process. The process you're going to do next will do the heavy lifting of clarifying what's helping and hindering effective priority-setting for you. Trust the process and seek to identify the one action you can take to either minimize an opposing force or accentuate a promoting force. Either one will be beneficial.

Yes, I said just *one action*. When you make it a priority to take one action on a daily basis to grow as a leader, you'll accelerate your learning and identify what works and what doesn't and then take another follow-up action. You'll rinse and repeat and by doing so you'll grow as a leader.

Force-Field Analysis

A force-field analysis is a commonly used and helpful tool used in many organizations. Specifically, they help leaders and teams identify the forces that support and hinder their ability to complete a project or achieve an objective.

Opposing Barriers

What are the opposing barriers to fulfilling your promises? These can be people, processes, or available resources. Brainstorm the longest list possible. For you as a leader, a force-field analysis can be helpful in identifying the factors that hinder you from achieving your purpose. Some examples could be spending too much time in unproductive meetings or serving on too many committees outside of work.

Promoting Forces

What are the promoting forces that can ensure your promises and purpose are lived out successfully? These too can be people, processes, or available resources. An example could be a passion for customer experiences or helping employees flourish. A force-field analysis will help you answer the following questions:

1. What is the ultimate promise, goal, or objective I want to achieve?
2. What are all of the opposing or promoting forces of my promise?
3. What is the priority ranking I'd give to each of the forces?
4. What forces are the most important and need addressing immediately?
5. What are my most important actions to take?

6. When will I schedule these actions for implementation?
7. Who will I ask to be my accountability partner and when will I meet with them to discuss my responses with them?

Priority-Setting in Real Time

There's an old adage: When you fail to plan, you plan to fail. In the work you've done here you've identified where your priorities are aligned and misaligned with your purpose. That begs the question: What do you do now?

Without overly simplifying priority-setting and minimizing the urgent matters you'll face every day, the most important next step you can take is to choose where you will invest time and energy to fulfill your purpose. Priorities get your time and attention, so knowing where you want to invest your time and energy is important, especially since in the next principle we'll address doing work and projects that are transformational for you and your organization.

Have you articulated your promises? Can you see a direct linkage between your promises and your purpose? Are there one or two promises that, if you were to more fully live it/them out, it would have a positive impact on the people who matter most to you? Is there a promise that, if you made it and it became a priority for you, you would experience a greater sense of satisfaction and well-being? What one step will you take to make it become real today? That's the place you start.

3

The Projects Principle

Projects As a Leadership Development Exercise

Unfortunately, in many organizations the word *project* creates a negative response. Too many projects are cumbersome and lumbering. They're populated with people who view the project as a time suck and who lack creativity and enthusiasm for doing meaningful work. Also, because they feel over scheduled, overworked, and overwhelmed, they want to check off the project team meeting on their to-do list and go back to more important work. What is perceived is the belief that projects are a waste of time as opposed to a vehicle for creating high-value, meaningful, fun, and transformational work.

There are two ways we can think about the word projects: The first way is to think of the word as a noun and in a project management–type of way. Using the word this way pertains to planning and designing work so a positive result can be achieved. It refers to a research project, for example. Leaders tend to like projects in this sense as it implies that meaningful work is being pursued, and with the right project management skills, success can be achieved.

The second way to think about the word *project* is as a verb. Here the word is rooted in extending outward, beyond something else, as in a movie being projected onto a 50-foot-wide screen. Projects in this sense are synonymous with magnifying and extending beyond an originating source.

The third principle in transformational leadership is more concerned with how you as a leader project your purpose, promises, and priorities into the conversations, meetings, emails, and presentations that comprise your everyday life. It is an invitation to design and implement a leadership development project that rapidly, ruthlessly, and relentlessly projects who you are as a leader into the world of work.

The metaphor I find helpful to position your leadership project is that of a light bulb. Think about two light bulbs. The first is a 100-watt bulb used in any room of your house. Most people think of the bulb in terms of wattage, but what is equally, if not more important is the brightness of the bulb, or its lumens. The 100-watt bulb you have in close proximity to where you are sitting has, on average, 1,600 lumens.

Compare that to a drive-in movie theater light bulb. The light bulb used to project a movie onto a 50-foot-wide screen from 150 feet away requires a bulb with between 33,000 and 40,000 lumens. The greater the lumens the farther the image can be projected.

The same holds true for your leadership project. The more lumens, or love and passion for your project, the farther you can project it to a broader audience. But as with either a light bulb at home or a drive-in movie theater, preparations must be made before the light bulb can be turned on. In this section you will clear the decks of any outdated project-related thinking and replace it with the thinking necessary to be successful. Implementing the following strategies allows you to be successful faster and with greater satisfaction. For your leadership project to be transformational there are five strategies you'll want to embrace.

Strategy #1: Act Smaller

The number-one problem people run into when it comes to doing transformational work is that they get caught up in the urgencies of the day and lose sight of the one small thing they can do today to achieve their bigger tomorrow. I'm not suggesting you think small in relation to what you want to accomplish or what you're capable of. What I am suggesting is that you need smaller daily actions that, when repeated over and over again, result in the accomplishment of your transformational project.

As a former triathlete, I learned to think of my year-long training programs in four-week and quarterly time frames. For a half-Ironman distance triathlon (a 1.2-mile swim, a 56-mile bike ride, and a 13.1-mile run) I held the picture of a completed triathlon in a particular time and placement loosely in my mind's eye, but held tightly to the four weeks of training in front of me. The process is called *periodization*. The process involves three weeks of building the intensity and duration of your training followed by one week of recovery time. This process is proven to help you go longer and faster, with less injury.

Transformational leadership projects are the same. For you to be successful, hold loosely to the vision of transforming a particular area of your business, but hold tightly to the small next steps required to be successful throughout the next four weeks and the next quarter. This process allows you to have multiple wins or successes, as well as create a higher sense of urgency and focus.

Strategy #2: Master Your Mindset

My personal trainer once told me that how I look physically has more to do with what I put in my mouth than it does with my exercise routine. He reminded me that the time I spend doing cardio and weight training is fruitless if I eat chocolate cake, potato chips, and pizza. He smiled and said, "It's a losing strategy to expect six-pack abs if you eat that way." I did not like hearing that bad news.

Transformational leaders choose carefully the thoughts they allow to permeate their thinking and master the internal dialogue they have with themselves.

They jettison negative "I can't do this" types of narratives, and replace them with "I'm smart and will learn how to do this" types of thinking. This is not a Pollyanna perspective, nor is it looking at the world through rose-colored glasses. It is a highly pragmatic and practical process for supplying your project with the nutritionally dense thinking that allows you to be successful. If you would like to learn 27 strategies for doing this more fully, you can download my complimentary "Mastering Your Mindset" special report at *www.clarisconsulting.net*.

Strategy #3: Cultivate Ruthless Focus

When your leadership project is compelling to you it's easy to focus on it, especially when all is well at work and home. But when the yogurt hits the fan it's far more difficult. That's when a ruthless focus on your project is required. The demands of your day will do all they can to take you off course, so you must have a clear and compelling reason for completing your leadership project. You will learn more strategies in the Perseverance Principle, but even before designing your leadership project it's important to know your project will get derailed and you'll find people who will want you to set priorities that are important to them and less important to your projects. That's when a ruthless, make-no-excuses focus is essential.

Strategy #4: Create White Space

We are a hyper-connected culture. We are connected to our bosses, our employees, and our colleagues through our smartphones and email. A Gallup panel survey conducted in April and May of 2015 showed that 81 percent of adults have a smartphone within reach during their waking hours, and 80 percent of those who have the phone in close proximity check their phone "a few times per hour." This leaves you more reactive than proactive.

The white space I'm suggesting is a 15-minute block of time once before you start your day and once before you end your day. This is a time where you unplug, disconnect, and take an inventory of what's working and what's not working, with regard to your leadership, your team, and your results. For example, the questions my clients might ask at the end of the day are:

1. What success or successes am I most grateful for today?
2. What specifically did I do that helped me be successful, and what can I do to leverage this success for even greater successes and satisfaction?
3. Where did I come up short today?
4. What specifically did I do that resulted in me not being successful, and what patterns or themes am I seeing that need my attention?
5. What will I do differently tomorrow?

6. What help, if any, will I need tomorrow to be successful?

Strategy #5: Hire a Coach

We cannot tell ourselves the unvarnished truth nor can we grow as fast and with heightened consistency without a coach. Leadership is not a solo activity and leaders must have followers in order to be effective. Leaders also need someone they trust and respect to tell them the truth and to provide an outsider's perspective. In turn, coaches and mentors can be catalysts for accelerated performance. Nowadays, athletes have coaches, musicians have coaches or teachers, and CEOs have coaches. Coaches are truth-tellers who say what we need to hear in ways we can hear it. Without an outsider's perspective we will hold on to biased perspectives.

Know this before you head into the next section: These five strategies, when coupled with a project you'd love to accomplish, ensure your success.

Focusing on Inputs Is a Career-Limiting Move

The first and most important step in developing a transformational leadership project is forgetting your methodology and your prior experiences with projects. When you forget methodology, what you'll end up with at the end of this chapter is not the same old project. This may not be easy for you, as we are indoctrinated to believe that what we do is vitally important, and doing it well leads us to success. However, that is not true.

For 10 years I worked as a financial advisor to high-net-worth software executives. For the first two years after entering the business I was predominantly focused on the methodology required to manage money success-fully. That's not a bad idea when it comes to managing someone's money, but my focus came from spending time with academic and theoretical brainiac invest-ment advisors who were partnering with the compliance department to ensure no one got sued, especially the firm I worked for.

What I believed and projected to my clients was that my method of managing a portfolio was so compelling that no one could resist the logic and would, if they were smart, hire me as their advisor. I was so enamored with my methodology that I neglected to become enamored with what really mattered to the client: helping them achieve their most important financial objectives. Quite frankly, I was more interested in the transactional aspects of port-folio construction than I was in the transformational aspects of accomplishing a client's hopes and dreams.

After leading with methodology and being mar-ginally successful, I learned a value-based conversation that shoved methodology to the back burner and placed focusing on client value front and center. It was a simple conversation I had with clients that started with "What's important about money to you?" What I learned by ask-ing value-based questions was astounding.

In my first conversation with a couple (the husband was a physician who earned more than seven figures per year), I heard important items mentioned from the husband, such as return on investment, reducing their tax liability, investing in down markets, and choosing the best investment vehicles. His wife gave a completely different answer. She gave a one-word answer that projected her greatest priority: *security*. For 10 minutes she told me how insecure she felt because they had not executed a will, there was no life insurance policy that named her as the beneficiary, and her husband's ex-wife was still on the title for their home after eight years.

With tears streaming down her face she said, "If anything happens to him I'll be a bag lady." The husband said that was ridiculous, but for her the reality was staring her in the face and had been for eight years. Without planning and an outsider's help they would repeat what they had done for the last eight years. What she wanted more than anything was a financial lifeline that would eliminate the uncertainty, apprehension, and angst associated with their management of money.

I would never have learned what was really important unless I jettisoned my focus on what I did (methodology) and instead focused on the highest of priorities: the results that the client wanted.

Let's cut to the chase: No one cares about modern portfolio theory and portfolio optimization other than industry professionals. What people care about is what modern portfolio theory and portfolio optimization gives them. They are simply tools or a means to the end of using financial resources in ways that make people feel secure, happy, and confident that their financial lives are in order. Can modern portfolio theory and portfolio optimization help people achieve their goals? Of course. Is every financial advisor using both as tools to make clients successful financially? Yes, every single one.

But what transformational leaders know is that what compels someone to say yes to their ideas is not the tools used. Have you ever asked a dentist what type of drill he will use to complete a filling? Have you ever asked a mechanic what tools he will use to repair your car? Can you imagine hiring a remodeling contractor based on what tools they use? I'll bet you nine times out of 10 your decision is based on the level of trust and respect you have for the contractor and whether you believe they have the ability to produce the result you want. In my case, when someone felt I cared less about my methodology and what was interesting or important to me, and instead my primary goal was to help them live the most rewarding and enriching financial life, my practice doubled in revenue in 24 months.

What You Should Focus On

The case I'm making is simple: If you are a financial advisor, accountant, attorney, engineer, IT professional, in human resources, or in any technically trained profession, you need to fall out of love with what you do and fall in love with making your clients', customers', and employees' lives better for having worked with you. Falling in love with making other's lives easier and more rewarding is then projected onto the mental screen held in between the ears of your customers and it says, "This person can improve the quality of my life." For that message to be received the nature and tone of your conversations needs to change from how you do what you do to what is important to them. To get to the real motivation people have for saying yes to you and your ideas, the following types of questions are essential.

Results

1. What is the most important goal or objective you want to accomplish?
2. What is important to you about accomplishing that?
3. How would life be better if you accomplished this objective?
4. If you could set priorities for what must be accomplished throughout the course of the next three to 12 months, what must happen for you to feel successful and satisfied?
5. What has been your experience in working toward this goal previously? What worked for you, what didn't, and what must happen for you to know you are successful?

Metrics

1. What will you want to see in order to know you are making progress toward your goal?
2. What is acceptable achievement, and what is ideal achievement?
3. Who would you like involved in measuring progress?
4. How specifically will you measure progress?

Value

1. What's important about this to you personally?
2. What would be the difference if you were supremely successful?
3. What would happen if you were completely unsuccessful? What would that mean to you?
4. What is not having this goal accomplished costing you now personally, professionally, financially, and emotionally?

Notice that there is nothing in the conversation regarding how I would go about helping someone accomplish the result they want. The only thing I'm interested in is learning as much as I can about what's important to the other person. I want to know their hopes, fears, aspirations, and desires. When I know what's important I learn what priorities should be adopted and the best way to accomplish them.

The previous questions serve two purposes: First, they help you learn what's important to other people so you can help them. Second, they guide you in thinking through a transformational leadership project for yourself. Your leadership development project is clarified when you start with the question "What's the most important goal or objective I want to accomplish as a leader?" The results to each of the questions point you to a leadership project that integrates everything you've learned thus far. Your job after answering these questions is to ensure your project is aligned with your purpose, has clear promises, and stipulates non-negotiable priorities to be successful.

If your methodology is front and center, a client's hopes, dreams, and aspirations will take a back seat. If your methodology is front and center, your leadership will be transactional and not transformational. Do transformational leaders have a process and methodology for doing exemplary work? Absolutely.

The questions you'll want answers to after having read this section are:

- "What am I projecting as a leader?"
- "Am I leading a purpose-centric life or an accidental life?"
- "Am I making people's lives easier or more difficult?"

Once you fall in love with your clients' or employees' hopes, dreams, and aspirations, you'll learn how to create a flourishing bottom line.

A Flourishing Bottom Line Requires Flourishing Employees and Customers

Stop and think about the word *flourishing* for a moment. The definition of the word is: "to grow well or luxuriantly, to thrive, to do or fare well, to prosper, to be in a period of highest productivity, excellence, or influence, to make bold, sweeping movements."

Are you faring well, prospering, highly productive, excelling, and living boldly? Are your employees faring well, prospering, being more productive, excelling, and living boldly? Are your customers faring well, prospering, being more productive, excelling, and living boldly after having worked with you? Would your employees give similar answers to yours? Would your customers answer in similar ways?

My experiences with my most successful clients is that their personal levels of prosperity, excellence, boldness, and sweeping movements are passed along to employees without any increases. When leaders aren't flourishing there are no employees flourishing. And we know where that leads with customers.

When employees are simply surviving, and are unproductive and committed to the status quo rather than excellence, they will be reticent if not resentful to the idea of customer flourishing. When leaders are not flourishing they cannot become exemplars and catalysts for those around them to flourish.

There is a very simple prism through which transformational leaders view their role and responsibility as leaders. They see their job through what I call The Flourishing Performance Formula, which has three key parts:

1. **A leader's job is to ensure the design, creation, and implementation of flourishing customer experiences.** You'll know you've accomplished this when customers voluntarily and repeatedly use your products and services even in the face of price increases. You'll know it when you see customers refer new customers to you. You'll hear things such as, "The CEO of Northwest Design told me I had to call you." These will not be one-off comments. Comments like these happen repeatedly when customers are flourishing. You'll also see customers not only remain open and receptive to your ideas and new products, but they'll call and ask you for your advice before taking action.

2. **A leader's job is to ensure the design, creation, and implementation of flourishing employee experiences that achieve key #1.** You'll know you've accomplished this when employees willingly and enthusiastically discuss and brainstorm ways to create excellent customer value and experiences. To that end

you'll see continual experimentation, learning, and growth along with heightened levels of accountability for doing so. There is continual praise and celebration for a job well done by all teams and team members as well as an overarching commitment to making one customer's and one employee's life easier and more rewarding daily.

3. **A leader's job is to ensure they personally flourish in order to create key #1 and key #2.** The apple doesn't fall far from the tree. If you as a leader desire to lead an organizational transformation you cannot do so without an individual leadership transformation taking place with all leaders. If you want greater accountability are you the exemplar and avatar for accepting accountability? If you know that letting go of past successes is essential for the accomplishment of new successes, do people point to you as the epitome of not resting on your laurels? Are you in a continual state of learning, growth, excelling, high productivity, prosperity (not financially per se), and living a bold and flourishing life? If you are not, it is disingenuous for you to ask others to do so.

The simplicity of this formula can come across as overly basic for sophisticated, hard-charging MBA types and it can be easily dismissed. But in leadership, especially with respect to the idea of customer and employee flourishing, leaders who minimize the idea of human flourishing do so at their peril.

Before you read the next paragraph, rate yourself on a 1 to 5 scale, with 5 being the highest manifestation of flourishing and 1 being the lowest, regarding the three questions. If you're a 3 on any question, what is the likelihood you can create a rating higher than that for your employees and customers? Very low.

There are two key points this chapter will make. The first is that a focus on customer and employee flourishing will not only increase your performance, but will dramatically increase your level of personal satisfaction and enjoyment with work. Secondly, when a leader wants to transform her or his organization, a personal leadership transformation is required first. Rest assured, my experience with successful leaders is that a leader's purpose, promises, and priorities can be game-changers that lead to her or him flourishing. When you integrate all of the work you've done so far with the idea of flourishing you'll accomplish results that are described as "transformational" by the people who matter most to you.

Why Is Flourishing in Short Supply?

Flourishing is in short supply quite simply because of lowered standards. Customers have become accustomed to airlines that regularly delay flights and dismiss passenger frustration; they've come to expect banks and other financial institutions to be more concerned with the bank's financial well-being than the customers. (The fraudulent account debacle at Wells Fargo in 2016 is an example.) Also, the national political narrative has been degraded to unimaginable levels. Every presidential election since the founding of our republic has had contentious and divisive elections. In 1800, when Thomas Jefferson and John Adams faced off against one another (one was the sitting president and the other vice president), the election got so nasty that after the election Congress passed the 12th Amendment, which disallowed the nominee with the second-most number of votes to be elected vice president. Politics has and will likely retain a common narrative: Each candidate is a barrier to America flourishing, each is unethical and/or immoral, each is inept as a leader and, if elected, America will be flushed down the toilet.

The negative experience associated with lower standards has become so prevalent that many customers are simply waiting to be disappointed and are looking for the slightest interruption to an expectation as proof that organizations don't care about them. Customers have become jaded and distrusting, which means organizations have to create new experiences that counteract this prevailing mindset. But employees oftentimes feel the same way and a victimization mindset has taken root in many corners of American society. Leaders are facing headwinds of unprecedented proportions that start in between the ears and behind the eyes of employees as well as customers.

Flourishing is a mindset issue. The subtitle of this book is *Create a Mindset of Passion, Innovation, and Growth*. The operative word is *mindset*. I've been studying mindset for more than 20 years and have found that mindset trumps skill set and is the key differentiator for my most successful clients. It will sound counterintuitive to the denizens of servant leadership, but I believe a leader's first job is to flourish personally and professionally in order to be an exemplar and role model to others. I don't mean this as an invitation to be self-centered, narcissistic, greedy, and an egocentric leader. It is instead recognition that leaders who flourish with the intent of enabling others to flourish are a magnet for transformational results.

Flourishing Recommendations

Flourishing requires you to embrace three mindsets: the flourishing customer, the flourishing employee, and flourishing leadership.

1. Embrace the Flourishing Customer Mindset

Leaders who create transformational results are clear about the mindset they want their customer to have after doing business with them. They have thought about and articulated clearly what each customer will feel, think, know, believe, and do. They then turn these desired experiences into designed experiences. This is similar to what Walt Disney did while opening his first theme park. He and his team thought through each aspect of a guest experience and designed delight into every step. There wasn't a building, ride, or guest experience that wasn't choreographed. Transformational leaders do the same.

How do customers feel after having completed an interaction or transaction with your team or organization? Do they feel empowered, smart, savvy, part of the in crowd, hip, or effective? Have you made their lives easier? Name the three most important experiences you want a customer to have with and through you or your company. Then go and ask three of your best clients for three words that best describe their experience with you. Is it the same, close, or nowhere close to what you desired? What you will learn in this one small section is essential to a flourishing business, so take your time to answer the questions from your perspective and then talk with a client.

Embrace the Flourishing Employee Mindset

You've heard the admonition that never a happy customer has been created with an unhappy employee. There is a myriad of reasons why you may have unhappy employees, but it boils down to two primary reasons: You either inherited them or you created them. In both cases, leaders are required to do something to reverse the situation.

On a flight across the country I overheard two flight attendants loudly discussing their new contract from the galley. Being only two rows removed from their conversation the vitriol and negativity was palpable, and the five-and-a-half hours being exposed to the surly flight attendants was such that when possible I fly another airline.

What mindset do you want your employees to hold about your customer and you as a leader? Do you want employees to feel that the customer experience has to be one of flourishing, otherwise you're failing? Do you want employees to see you as trustworthy, persistent, honest, inspiring, visionary or strategic? What do you want employees to know you stand for? And based on these ideals, what do you want them to do? When you think about the customer experience and the mindset needed by employees to create it, what needs to be in place now that currently is not in place?

Leaders get clear about what kind of employee mindset is required in order to create the desired customer mindset. By that I mean leaders get very specific about the behaviors, attitudes, and thought processes an employee will cultivate in order to create the customer experience. Without this level of clarity employees are driving in the fog and likely to careen off the road and take the customer out with them.

Embrace the Flourishing Leadership Mindset

It is a fool's errand to think for a moment that the customer and employee mindset will come alive by a leader who, in their heart of hearts, is dead to the idea of flourishing experiences for employees and customers. Consider the word *inspiration*, for example. The word comes from the Latin root *inspire*, which means "to breathe life into something." To breathe life into something, the life has to first be inside you. In overly simplistic terms, you can't give CPR if you are dead.

If you are convinced that flourishing is the ideal for your customers and your employees, the next section on leadership development will provide you with the framework for seeing your leadership project as a laboratory for flourishing.

It's Not What You Know, It's What You Can Teach

Far too often leaders feel overwhelmed by the everyday demands of their jobs and they in turn disengage from the ideal of employees flourishing and doing their best work. They love the idea of employee flourishing and of a flourishing bottom line, but are not actively engaged in a leadership project that allows it to happen.

Why is that? Most leaders I meet in organizations come to work and want to do good work and they want to make a difference, but they allow themselves to get overwhelmed by their to-do list, become highly transactional, and lose sight of what drives employee enthusiasm for doing their best work. They allow the naysayers and negative nellies to convert their thinking from possibility-based thinking to probability-type thinking.

The truth about leadership is that strong leaders become transformational leaders; leaders who want to do their best work, and who want others to do their best work, surround themselves with transformational employees. Transformational leaders are not intimidated by smart, talented, and driven employees. On the contrary, they are emboldened and relentless about surrounding themselves with the brightest and best.

Transformational leaders fully recognize that transformational employees need and seek opportunities to learn, grow, and expand their skill set as well as their mindset. They are never content to simply maintain the status quo. When their rhythm of work becomes too repetitive and the results become predictable, transformational employees will create new opportunities where they are or will leave and seek them elsewhere.

Weak leaders, on the other hand, surround themselves with weak employees. Weak leaders feel as though they must keep employees from surpassing them and are afraid of having employees show them up. They in turn surround themselves with people who are content where they are and are less interested in learning, growth, and innovation.

Let me be clear: Your leadership project will help you implement what you have learned so you can be a strong and transformational leader. Your project is the primary tool you use for internalizing and personifying all that you have learned while illuminating the path for other employees to follow.

It is worth repeating: With a compelling and virtuous purpose, clear promises, and strategic priorities that support you and your employees doing their best work, your leadership project will help you not only accomplish your business results, but also make a positive difference in the lives of the employees. This in turn makes a positive difference in the lives of your customers. By helping your employees live a more rewarding and enriching life, your project will be transformed from a boring, mind-numbing, and draining type of project into the projection of something valuable and important.

There were two strong and transformational leaders that transformed my thinking at an early age and who set the stage for allowing me to do my best work. The first was my junior high school track coach, David Litton. In one gym class he saw me beat the running-back of the football team in three, 40-yard dashes. Although the football coach felt threatened that some skinny kid with no talent or interest in football would embarrass his star player, Coach Litton saw something different. He saw in me the raw talent for running fast and painted a picture for me of having the same type of success as the football players, but in a sport that played to my strengths. When I said yes to joining the track team, Coach Litton coached me physically and psychologically to be a star athlete in my own light. He invested time in helping me to be the best version of me I could be.

Billie James, my high school guidance counselor, recognized the difficulty I was having with school, friends, and family. One morning, she woke up thinking about me and what she could do to help me adjust to the challenges. At 3 a.m. she wrote me a five-page letter telling me about all the strength and goodness she saw in me. She entitled the letter "Prizing Hugh." Billie believed in me and saw talents and skills I couldn't see. She went above and beyond what I thought was the traditional boundary of high school counselor and left an indelible mark on my personal and educational life.

Both David and Billie infused into my thinking a much-needed confidence, hope, and optimism. Thirty-five years later the seeds planted by David and Billie have deep roots. From them I learned that caring for another person is the first step in changing his or her thinking. If I didn't feel that David or Billie cared for me I would not have been receptive to their ideas of what they thought might be possible for me.

In our busy and fractured lives, we have the same choice as Billie and David: to shed light into those areas that remain darkened to new possibilities, to plant seeds of hope where there is despair, and grow optimism where there is uncertainty and fear. If we do these things, there is a corresponding increase in a person's well-being and willingness to exert themselves to achieve a new and bigger potential. The moment the seeds of optimism

and hope are planted in the world of work, the potential for increased productivity and profitability increases
proportionately.

How can you do the same? I'll use the word *light* as
a pneumonic for how Billie and David positively influenced me and how you too can positively influence others. Light stands for:

Listening. Billie and David listened to understand
and not simply to respond. They suspended any judgment of what I said and were fully present to my fears,
hopes, complaints, and concerns. Every young adult
wants to know that they have been listened to and understood. Sure, our parents listen to us and want the best for
us, but all too often in their hope of making us strong
young adults they listen to respond as opposed to listen
to understand. With Billie and David I left most conversations feeling valued, important, and heard.

Integrity. David and Billie aligned their values with
their behavior. John Wooden, the famed UCLA basketball coach, once said, "Sports doesn't build character—it
reveals it." This quote was later changed to a leadership
context and read, "Adversity doesn't build character—it
reveals it." When I think back to how Billie and David
acted toward me I can unquestioningly see alignment
between what they said they believed and what they
did; there was alignment and I saw them as credible and
trustworthy.

Generosity. Billie and David were generous people.
In their roles both had lots of kids to look after and yet

they still found time to let each child know he or she was important and valued. In the midst of all they had going on I never felt rushed when talking with them. I don't think they thought about it as being generous, they were simply being themselves. And in the midst of their generosity toward me I learned how to be generous also. At 12 years old I didn't call it gratitude. I called it "nice" and "cool."

At my 30-year high school reunion I spoke with Billie and expressed my gratitude for her caring letter. She did not remember the letter, but was touched by what she called my "generous memory." My conversation with Billie was a transformational conversation for me. I saw, maybe for the first time, how throughout the arc of a life one letter or conversation can positively impact a person. Her generosity planted the seed of generosity in me that still grows today.

Heart-to-heart connection. David and Billie built relationships based on love, care, and resonance. They genuinely cared about the children they taught and saw each child's hopes, dreams, and aspirations as fragile and worthy of their attention. They purposefully planted the seed of courageousness in me and cultivated the belief that with focus, hard work, and discipline, my hopes, dreams, and aspirations were possible.

Telling the truth. Billie and David didn't pull any punches. They told me what I needed to hear, but did so in a way I could hear it. In hindsight, I think they were master communicators. I've met people who say that they are "brutally honest" and believe this is virtuous. I've found them to have more brutality in their message than honesty, but that is because how they deliver their message is done in ways that work for them and not for the person with whom they are speaking. Telling someone what they need to hear in ways they can hear it involves being grounded in wanting to be generous, aligning your behavior with your values, and listening to the other person in order to know how best to talk with them.

It's really quite simple: Performance, innovation, growth, and commitment deteriorate when leaders lose sight of their role of making a positive difference in the lives of those they lead or manage. Having an appreciable increase in the performance, innovation, and collaboration within your team and organization requires a generous focus on shedding light in all of your personal interactions. By shedding light, you will transform your employees' hopes and aspirations for work into something real and tangible.

Cascading Excellence Throughout Your Organization

There is a common misconception that people resist change. I disagree. A good friend and colleague once said, "People don't mind change. What they mind is feeling badly." If a leadership project and/or change initiative will leave employees feeling incompetent, dumb, or lazy they will resist the change. They may agree with the necessary changes, but by adopting the changes they end up feeling inferior or incompetent. The change will stall and accelerated performance is all but impossible.

Does this mean leaders must become therapists and walk through their organization asking people how they "feel" about a change? Yes and no. I'm not recommending for a moment that leaders emulate the television therapist Dr. Phil. You're off the hook in that regards. However, I am recommending that if you want transformational levels of growth, understanding how the change impacts employees and stakeholders—how the change makes them feel—must be recognized, respected, reflected on empathically, and responded to accordingly. When a leader cannot talk about how people are faring during the change, they are seen as out of touch, clueless, or disinterested. Employees are merely cogs in the wheel.

When a leader can discuss the emotional parts of change and how people are faring, employees and stakeholders feel heard and valued, and are open to hearing a leader's thoughts on the next steps. They are active listeners to the following three cascading communication strategies.

1. **Defining the "what."** Leaders must answer *what* it is that must be accomplished. Leaders are required to paint a compelling image of the future that is exciting, ennobling, uplifting, and compelling.
2. **Articulating the "why."** Leaders must also present unassailable reasons *why* the attainment of

the future is in everyone's best interests. The *why* portion of cascading excellence touches both the head and the heart of employees and leaves them saying, "Yes, you're right."

3. **Partnering on the "how."** Employees and stakeholders who have a voice, are asked for advice, and are allowed to have their finger-prints all over a project plan or change ini-tiative view the change as their idea and will make promises and set priorities that foster its accomplishment.

Why Individual Transformation Matters

If leaders want an organizational transformation they have to be prepared to undergo an individual transfor-mation first. It's so simple, but oftentimes overlooked. What a leader does every day communicates what is important to her. Has she made promises to continu-ally learn new ways of helping customers and employees flourish? Does she have priorities that create high value for her stakeholders?

If leaders want to cultivate organizational excellence they must first cultivate individual excellence. It is dis-ingenuous at best to pronounce employee and customer excellence as an aspiration that is non-negotiable, and then to live in ways that support maintaining the status quo. Let's not mince any words. If you want to cascade excellence into every customer and employee experience, you as a leader must embrace pursuing personal and professional excellence.

Leaders are role models for change, growth, innovation, and transformation. Their every move and conversations are being watched and, in turn, are an opportunity to live out their purpose, promises, and priorities. If this makes you nervous, it should, but there is good news. Employees are not looking for perfection. They are looking for someone who instills confidence, courage, and clarity about helping them to flourish, do their best work, and make their lives easier. Exhibiting these aspirations garners tremendous good will and fosters a partnership with leaders to cascade excellence throughout an organization.

Your Transformational Leadership Project

Every organization has deep reservoirs of talent that are not achieving their full potential. There are many reasons why full potential is not achieved and excellence is not cascaded throughout an organization. You will no doubt have your own list, but after working with organizations for 30-plus years I have found a set of 20 reasons why talent is not realizing its full potential. Here is my list. What would you add?

1. Uninspiring leadership.
2. Unclear expectations.
3. Low levels of trust and respect.

4. A culture of compliance rather than commitment.
5. A lack of, or a continually changing, strategic direction.
6. Low levels of accountability.
7. The wrong performance metrics.
8. The creation and tolerance of disengaged employees.
9. Low levels of critical/objective thinking.
10. Poor or no strategic prioritization and decision-making.
11. Low levels of rewards and recognition.
12. A lack of disciplined execution.
13. No fun.
14. Little or no coaching or mentoring.
15. The wrong people in the wrong role.
16. No process for continually overcoming barriers.
17. A negative mindset.
18. Double standards: Senior leaders do one thing and expect another from the rank and file.
19. Seeing employees and customers as broken.
20. Unhappy customers based on inferior products or services.

Whether you work in a start-up company with 10 employees or a mature organization with 25,000 employees, cascading excellence throughout your organization requires leaders to engage in a continual leadership development process that is focused on talent maximization, barrier elimination, and results acceleration. In no uncertain terms this is what transformational leaders do. In this section you will design a holistic leadership development project and dive headlong into increasing your business performance.

Talent Maximization

Talent maximization starts with the premise that you have talented people working with you. If you don't, that's a separate management issue that will not be addressed here. But assuming you do, in order to convert the skills and talents of employees, you must identify the employees who are evangelists for what you want to accomplish. These employees have the mindset and skill set that is not only supportive of your leadership, but enthusiastic and committed.

Think about your project and clarify who should be involved. Who represents the best mindset, the best skill set, the best experience, the greatest passion, the greatest energy, and the greatest creativity? Name your top three or five people and what talent they bring to the project.

Barrier Elimination

You can have the smartest and hardest-working employees on the planet, but they will never produce accelerated business results if the one and only thing standing in between them and greater results is not eliminated: barriers and obstacles.

Barriers can be cultural, process-oriented, attitudinal, communication-related, leadership, compensation, and so on. In order to cascade excellence throughout your organization, you should be less interested in the symptoms of lower performance, and more focused on the root causes that, once identified, help organizations remove barriers permanently.

Once you have identified the talent you want or need to achieve your project, it's time to enlist them in conducting a force-field analysis to break down the restraining forces to your leadership project or building on the promoting forces for achieving breakthroughs. As a reminder, restraining and promoting forces are:

Restraining Forces: What are the opposing barriers to a satisfying and successful completion of your project? These can be people, processes, or available resources. You'll want to brainstorm the longest list possible with your evangelists.

Promoting Forces: What are the promoting forces that can secure a satisfying and successful completion of your project? These can be people, processes, or available resources. Identifying your restraining and promoting forces requires that you address the following:

1. What is the result I want to achieve? This is the foundational question for your leadership project.

2. What are the metrics and value of completing my project?

3. What are the promoting and restraining forces that must be addressed?

4. How do I set priorities for the forces at play? Which needs addressing first, second, and third? Clarify and rank each one according to priority.

5. To what forces will I give immediate attention?

6. What new priorities and/or promises for my leadership are required in order for this project to be successful?

7. Where in my calendar will I schedule each aspect of my project?

Results Acceleration

The results you want in your leadership project must be infused with emotion. Yes, the "what" of the project must be clear, but the "why" must be fully present also. Without the emotion of the "why," the commitment necessary to do anything different or difficult will be absent.

Leaders must be the primary evangelist for their project. And although the word *evangelist* may have a negative connotation based on some political or religious intransigence, an evangelist is someone who builds a critical mass of belief, support, enthusiasm, and engagement for an idea or aspiration. In many ways, leaders have to balance being open and receptive to input with being single-minded, driven, and not taking no for an answer. They have to hit the street proclaiming what they believe and why it's important.

Results acceleration, especially when it comes to cascading excellence throughout an organization, requires an evangelical focus on the three dimensions of what was discussed in the Purpose Principle. It requires high levels of love, talent, and value. Leaders in turn link their strategic results and leadership project in ways that connect the love they have for their work, the talent they and others bring, and the value they are committed to creating.

I started this chapter recognizing that projects in the common usage had built a bad reputation. What I'll end with is the promise that with a compelling leadership purpose, high-value promises, and strategic priorities, you can design a leadership project that will not only provide transformational value to the people who matter most to you, but you can design a repeatable and enjoyable project that is more rewarding and enriching for you. In the next chapter, you learn how to persuade those with competing priorities to support your project using my three-part persuasion process.

4

The Persuasion Principle

Persuasion: What Is It and Do You Have It?

There are 1.7 million airline passengers on domestic flights in the United States every day. In order to board their flights, each passenger must proceed through a security screening process. This screening is done in the hopes of making traveling more safe and to verify that passengers are safe to proceed to their gate for departure.

For transformational leaders, they recognize that each of their stakeholders likewise has a screening process for listening to and following a leader's lead. This process is less about sharp objects and the two-ounce requirement for toiletries, but rather, is the leader safe to follow to the destination he advocates? If a leader doesn't pass the screening process he will not experience flashing lights or be asked to enter a small interrogation room, but will instead find himself at his departure gate perplexed as to why he is the only one on the flight to his desired future.

To *persuade* someone is defined by Merriam Webster as "causing someone to do something through reasoning or argument and to cause someone to believe something, especially after a sustained effort." Persuasion is therefore about convincing and influencing someone to act or think a certain way. The operative word is to *act*. In the face of competing demands, fewer resources, and higher expectations, leaders will encounter people who will not want to align their priorities with theirs.

Persuasion in transformational leadership is not about eloquent and stirring speeches like Abraham Lincoln's Gettysburg Address or Martin Luther King's I Have A Dream speech. Persuasion in transformational leadership is about positive influence, not manipulation. In its purest form persuasion is the shaping with full integrity the thoughts, feelings, beliefs, and behaviors of another. But that begs the question: Why do people do what they do? To know why people do what they do, you'll need to notice the order of the definition of persuasion, shaping the thoughts, feelings, beliefs, and behaviors of others. We're going to look at each aspect of persuasion specifically.

The key point you'll learn from the Persuasion Principle is that in order to have people behave in ways that are helpful to your purpose, promises, priorities, and projects, you must start by understanding and then shaping their thoughts, feelings, and beliefs about you and your initiatives so they will act in ways that are supportive of your requests. If you want to hear yes more often you have to know what happens in between people's ears before yes comes out of their mouths. If you don't understand what precedes yes you will continue to hear no.

Thoughts

Every action you and I take is preceded by a thought, and these thoughts are a powerful catalyst for how we live our lives and what we say yes to. In the TSA screening example, if your thoughts about TSA screening are that it is beneficial and helpful in making passengers safer, you will see airport screening in a positive light. If you think the process is a waste of time and neglects the bigger issue of screened baggage in the cargo bay, your thoughts regarding TSA screenings will lead you to see airport screening in a negative light.

Feelings

The thought that airport screening is valuable and increases the safety for all passengers is followed by the feeling of safety and or comfort. These feelings happen at light-speed and often go unnoticed. In reality, thoughts and feelings are highly interconnected. When you think your time is valuable and you strive to be expedient, an interference in being expedient is thought to be a threat and waste of time. The thought of having your time wasted creates a feeling of anxiety or apprehension for not being effective.

Beliefs

The beliefs we each hold for work, our stakeholders, and what we are capable of accomplishing are powerful triggers for our actions and behaviors. If I think airport screening is a waste of time and feel anxious for being hindered from doing my best work, my belief is that whatever obstacle I encounter needs to be avoided or eliminated. Setting aside the TSA example for a second, there are employees who have spectacular talent who don't believe in themselves and suffer from imposter syndrome. This belief holds that the person is not entitled to be in the position they are and that at some point the will be found to be an imposter. There are also leaders who believe they may not be the most talented leader, but they have the love and passion for what they do in such copious amounts that nothing will prevent them from achieving their goal. Whichever belief is held becomes true.

Behaviors

Here's the key point about behaviors: Whenever you see someone do something or act in a particular way, they are doing so because they believe the action they're taking is the best response to what they believe about a situation. If you see someone berating a TSA agent, they believe that by doing so they will secure the best outcome. You know this is foolhardy, but you are not feeling the same emotions nor are you having the same thoughts. Therein lies the great challenge for transformational leaders. The challenge is that if you want people to support your initiatives, say yes to your ideas, and support your purpose, priorities, projects, or promises, do not focus on the behaviors you're seeing. Focus on the thoughts, feelings, and beliefs driving the behavior.

At work, if a colleague sees you and her first thought is that you are political, manipulative, and lazy, that you are not a team player and that you are solely out for your own self-interests, the first feelings associated with seeing you would be that of dread. If I dread seeing you I have a self-preserving belief that I should extricate myself from a conversation with you as quickly as possible. The behavior you see from the other person may be described as curt, rude, and possibly dismissive. Transformational leaders then do behavioral jiujitsu. They ask themselves what beliefs, feelings, or thoughts are triggering these behaviors. They ask because when these questions are asked and answered the likelihood of hearing yes goes up appreciably.

So how persuasive are you? Put aside the theory of thoughts, feelings, beliefs, and behavior and ask yourself, "How persuasive am I? How persuasive is my leadership?" The simple answer is: If you're persuasive you'll hear four kinds of yes.

1. **Yes, that's a good idea, and yes I'll help.** This is the first and most potent yes. This is the most desired response leaders want, but frequently don't hear. For a leader to hear this yes they have given considerable thought to the priorities of the person they're asking, linked their proposal to the other person's self-interests, and found positive ways they can help the other person achieve a mutually rewarding end result.

2. **Yes, if we can add this one idea we can have an even more positive impact.** The second type of yes is one in which a second or complimentary idea is used to improve on your idea in a way that serves the greater purpose. When leaders hear this type of yes there is a creativity that is infused into the conversation. It is additive and builds on one idea and ultimately helps all involved to think bigger about the possible outcomes. This yes results in the idea no longer being the brain child of one person, but rather the collaborative idea of two or more people.

3. **Yes, I don't know how to do that, but I know I'll figure it out.** This yes can be a powerful and transformational yes. As leaders in

every organization can attest, there are objectives worth doing that don't have clear paths with well-lit signs and precise directions. And therein lies the positive side of leaders hearing this yes. Transformational leaders want to hear people say yes to their ideas, but maybe more importantly, they want to hear yes to ideas that challenge the status quo while cultivating a mindset of passion, innovation, and growth.

4. **Yes, I'll take care of it.** This yes is short and to the point and shows a clear agreement of what's requested. When a Chief Marketing Officer is asked to answer her board of directors questions—a board with little or no background in marketing—about how social media marketing is impacting the sales process, the best place to start is by understanding the thoughts the board has currently, what their feelings are about marketing and social media, as well as what, if any, beliefs are driving this request to be educated.

Hearing these four kinds of yes confirms that positive persuasion is underway and that you're on track to achieve your purpose, promises, priorities, and projects. That's the context of positive persuasion. In the next section you'll learn specifically the Transformational Leadership Persuasion Process.

The Three-Part Leadership Persuasion Process

If you are in a leadership position, you have likely read about how to have teams and employees you lead do something they may not want to do. A day does not go by that you don't directly or indirectly persuade someone. You have high hopes for having people follow your lead and act in ways that foster innovation, growth, and passion.

But in everyday life, leaders are dealing with the reality that, all too often, people don't do what they're asked and/or behave in ways that don't support the best interests of the customer, team, or organization.

Let's level set on one key issue. The employment journey, from on-boarding to exit interviews, is a persuasion process that sends a clear and compelling message to every employee about what's important and what the expectations are for doing transformational work. When leaders look at each interaction with employees and customers as a building block in the three-part persuasion process, it is simple to understand and remarkable in its effectiveness. In the three sections that follow we'll break down each part of the persuasion process and make it actionable and real world. The process of persuading another person is simple:

1. Build strong relationships based on trust and respect.
2. Understand the objectives and priorities of the other person.

3. Provide solutions that help them achieve their priorities.

If you do all three you'll have the persuasion necessary to lead the transformation of your project in powerful and compelling ways.

Why Trust and Respect Sound the Starting Gun

In order for you to become more persuasive, high levels of trust and respect are the foundational building block. Think for a moment about a colleague, boss, or teammate you don't trust or respect. How much positive persuasion does the person have with you? Likely very little. Trust is about doing what we say we will do and the corresponding credibility. Respect, on the other hand, is about having a high regard for the talents and skills of the other person.

Let's say you appoint a senior vice president (SVP) to lead a major project. In 2016, a major project would have been the Samsung recall of their Galaxy 7s phone. For those of you who don't remember, the phone caught fire and required every phone to be recalled. The recall eroded 26 billion ($26,000,000,000) yes, billion with a "B" worth of value. This was a high-stakes, if not life and death, situation for Samsung.

The SVP promised to complete a detailed analysis of the recall and present their findings to the board in 45 days. If the work presented is of a high standard and addresses all of the issues the board and executives raised, you will have a high regard for the SVP's skills and talents. If the work is accomplished in the promised timeframe, you see the SVP as trustworthy. In this case, trust and respect are both essential in order to persuade the senior executives and the board to stay the course and execute the developed plan.

Imagine, however, that the SVP meets their deadline, but submits work that is lacking in quality. Because the quality of the work is not respected, the SVP's ability to persuade the executives and board is compromised. The higher the stakes, the more important trust and respect become.

What's Important to You?

Knowing the objectives and priorities of the people you want to persuade is a crucial second step. This requires putting aside our own self-interests and prioritizing what is important to the other person. When we know what is important to the other person, for example, balancing the need for innovation and growth with the need to continually infuse excellence into products near the end of their life cycle, we can better present solutions that help achieve that objective.

In the Projects Principle we discussed jettisoning methodology in favor of results. The case I made was that falling out of love with what you do and falling in love with making your clients, customers, and employees lives better for having worked with you is a game-changing mindset shift. The same holds true in the Persuasion Principle. The act of falling in love with understanding the objectives and priorities of the people who can help or hurt your project, your career, and the resources you have, is an incredibly persuasive act. When the message you broadcast is one of "Your priorities are as important to me as they are to you," the quality of your relationships increases dramatically and leaves others not only open to what you have to say, but hopeful they can hear from you. You are now a strategic partner to the other person as opposed to the vendor or supplier of widgets.

Provide Solutions That Achieve Others' Priorities

The key point in this section is that when leaders lead with solutions without fully understanding and addressing the objectives and priorities of the person they want to persuade, it's the death knell for success even if you have the title of "CEO" after your name. The most successful leaders I've worked with tirelessly build the highest levels of trust and respect possible while immersing themselves in what's important to the other person before they ever suggest a solution.

In the three sections that follow we will take a deeper dive into the process and skills required to build high levels of trust and respect, know the objectives and priorities of others, and how to best provide solutions that leave people saying yes to your ideas.

Don't Raise Your Voice, Raise Your Persuasion IQ

The formula for building high levels of trust and respect is surprisingly simple: Do what you say you're going to do and do it to the agreed-upon standards. If you follow the formula you'll build trust and respect as well as have happy employees and customers. Wait a minute. If it's so simple why don't people do it? They don't do it for one primary reason: They think they've gotten clear about expectations when in reality they haven't. They lack a framework for getting clear and for infusing accountability into situations.

How are you doing with trust and respect? Here's a self-assessment to prompt your thinking as to how much positive persuasion you have. The following statements will ask you to rate yourself on the behaviors necessary to have high levels of trust and respect. On a scale of 1 to 10, with 10 being a high level of agreement and 1 representing a low level of agreement, rate yourself on the following statements.

Level of Trust

1. I actively and intentionally work to create an environment that fosters trust with my colleagues.
2. I do what I say I will do.
3. I act with integrity in all personal and professional interactions.

4. I speak well of people when they are not within earshot.

5. My colleagues say I genuinely care about each of them.

6. I tell the truth in ways that build trust.

Level of Respect

1. I look for and focus on my colleagues' talents and skills.

2. I frequently communicate my respect for the skills and talents my colleagues have.

3. I actively infuse as much value as possible into all of the interactions I have with colleagues.

4. I am focused and don't get distracted when interacting with my colleagues.

5. I feel respected by my colleagues.

6. I recognize and communicate my interest in and appreciation for others' perspectives.

Now, go back and answer the questions from the perspective of your boss, colleagues, or coworkers. How would they answer these questions about you? Do you see a gap between how you answered the questions and how you think your colleagues would answer the questions? Is there is a gap between your perception of your behavior and others' perceptions of your behavior? If so, there is a risk of having a credibility gap, which jeopardizes your ability to persuade others.

Quite simply, trust and respect is built on having clear expectations and doing what you said you would do.

Crafting Clear Expectations

Having clear expectations can reduce the strife in your personal life and professional life by 50 percent as well as increase your performance. You do that by getting clear about the expectations you have with someone. For example, a CEO client of mine led a $200,000,000 financial institution and was at loggerheads with the board as to their strategic direction and priorities. Her expectations were that growth and greater profitability would come from being a market-driven organization. This would lead to more time, money, and resources devoted to marketing to their key customers. If done well, the financials would continue to grow from their current positive place. The board had an expectation that they would be a financial-driven institution and that decisions would be rooted in the financials and that marketing needed to follow what the financials allowed.

These conflicting expectations required a higher level of clarity as to the fundamental expectations each party could agree on as well as expectations to address differing expectations in ways that built trust and respect. When I learned of the situation the CEO felt disrespected and undervalued and the board felt hindered from doing their job. Neither of the previous trust and respect questions would have rated the other highly on each dimension.

Clear expectations are rooted in seven fundamental steps.

1. Reaffirm the Purpose

In almost every frustrating situation I've experienced in board rooms and executive suites the one fatal flaw is jumping to how a situation can be resolved before clarifying the "what" or "why" of a situation. The process for establishing expectations that foster innovation, growth, and passion starts with the purpose of the team or organization. When you start a conversation with, "Our purpose is to dramatically improve the quality of our leadership while also dramatically increasing the quality of our business results," you have answered the overarching contextual question of what the purpose is. Yes, you may get wrapped around the proverbial axle when it comes to how to accomplish your purpose, but starting with what the purpose is points everyone in the right direction.

2. Define Success

The definition of success for your purpose and why it's beneficial infuses hope, optimism, and energy into the conversation. Someone may know what the intended purpose is, but until the definition of success is clarified for them individually the purpose will remain intellectual and theoretical. For example, if a leader in your organization hears that you want to dramatically increase the quality of the organization's leadership and her business results, she will likely say yes to that, as it's theoretically a sound idea. But the real power comes in articulating for each person the benefits of achieving the purpose. For example, if you accomplished your purpose you would achieve the following:

1. Leaders will have a clearer line of sight for career growth and no longer view their careers as unpredictable and unmanageable.
2. Leaders will have an accurate assessment of where they stand currently with specific successes to build on and targeted challenges to address.
3. Leaders will have professional development opportunities that, if taken advantage of, will propel them to higher levels of both success and satisfaction.

3. Clarify Roles, Responsibilities, and Time Frames

Next are the specifics of roles, responsibilities, and time frames. Each of these three areas need to be crisp, clear, and understood. For example, as Volunteer Coordinator, you are in charge of volunteer recruitment, development, retention, scheduling, and quality assurance (responsibilities) for the customer engagement project. My role will be to check in with you to ensure you have the most available resources and to see what I can do to help you be successful. Also, the kickoff of the project is six months from today and you'll have 15 hours per week away from your current work to devote to this. You're being asked to take on this role because of your expertise in managing volunteers and your success with the capital campaign last year. Addressing each area with specificity is required for someone to say yes to you.

4. Clarify Decision-Making

Imbedded in this step is the recognition of decision-making authority. Is a person able to make decisions unilaterally or only after conferring with their boss? Trust and respect are big parts of this step. If I trust and respect you, and have clearly articulated your role and budget, I may instruct you to make a decision you deem best to accomplish your purpose and to make us successful, and then the next time we meet tell me what you decided. This is delegation at its zenith. If the person in a role is a new employee with less experience I may ask for weekly status reports. Regardless of experience, clarify by using the following 1 through 5 decision-making model: 1 is, as the senior leader, I can and will make all of the decisions. I don't have to ask your opinion, but I do have to tell you; 2 is similar to a 1 except I will consult with you, ask for your opinion, and then make my decision; 3 is a mutual decision; 4 means you will make a decision after conferring with me; 5 means you can make a decision without conferring with me at all. If you do this one step alone any frustrations you have with expectation will go down by 50 percent.

5. Schedule Status Updates

This expectation is also directly rooted in trust and respect. If I have any uncertainty about your talents, skills, or ability to stay on task I may ask for more frequent status updates. You may also want more frequent status updates if the project is a mission critical project. In either case, knowing the frequency of the updates as well as what is expected in a status update is crucial. Saying, "Let's check in once every two weeks" lacks specificity. In this step, both parties can clarify what a status update looks like to them. For one person, it may be a percentage completed on high-priority tasks, actual to-budget figures, risk and challenges, and lessons learned. What's also required is what format the check-in will use. Will it be submitted in writing two days in advance so each person has time to digest the information and come prepared to ask questions? Be clear about what you want as well as what you can do given all of your other priorities.

6. Address the Issues

Issues that go unresolved will erode trust and respect quickly. It is essential for expectations to be meaningful and transformational. Without writing a chapter on conflict management, the best way to address issues is to ask a question with curiosity and openness. For example, "George, my understanding was that we agreed to check in once every two weeks and that you would have your status update circulated two days in advance of our in-person meeting. I didn't receive your update. Help me understand what happened." You'll likely hear a reasonable explanation and can discuss with George what to do moving forward. If you don't ask, George will know that there are no consequences for not circulating his report and will likely do the same again. The key is to recognize that you will erode trust and respect by not addressing the issues.

7. Confirm Understanding and Agreement

The final step is to confirm with the other person all of the previous steps. For example, "Based on this conversation let's check in that we're both on the same page. What do you understand your role, expectations, and the like to be?" When you have a clear summary you'll only have one next step. Go back to the Promises Principle section and review the priority setting section. Understanding how to go about creating clear expectations is one thing. The next is to set priorities around them so you can do what you promised the standard you agreed to. If you do, you'll have people more willing to say yes to your requests and you'll have fewer interruptions to higher performance.

You Have Two Ears and One Mouth

It has been said that the eyes are the window into the soul. If true, the ears are the doorway to the heart. It is by our ears we listen to what's important to someone. We not only hear the words they are using, but hear the tone of voice, inflection, and can distinguish between the emotions expressed and listen for what is hoped for moving forward. Our ears afford us the ability to do so, but all too frequently we don't. We are busy listening through the filter of what's important to us and in many cases don't listen, but interpret what others are saying.

One of my clients, Dr. Timothy Chester, is CIO at the University of Georgia and wrote an interesting blog that described the art of using our two ears and why one mouth is more than enough. He recounted a conversation he had with the director of human resources at Texas A&M University and how frustrating it was for them to talk with the IT director managing the university's payroll system. What human resources wanted was clear and authoritative data about employees. When human resources asked what some of the data meant, the response was, "What do you want the data to mean?"

There are two ways to view this conversation: The first is through the technical aspect of the conversation and how accurate and authoritative information is essential in making the best decision possible. The second is the people/persuasion prism and how imperative it is that technically trained and proficient professionals learn how to listen first in order to understand what's important to someone before opening their mouths. Then, as in the persuading process, our mouths can be used to provide significant value to the person we're speaking with, namely to help people be successful. When we use our ears first we have the potential of becoming a strategic business partner known for solving problems.

Throughout the last 15 years I've worked with hundreds of technically brilliant and well-intended professionals who are more accomplished at leaving their lesser technically inclined constituents frustrated rather than empowered. While they listen intently for the technical issues related to an issue, they turn a deaf ear to the people and relationship side of their work. In turn, they communicate their lack of a clear and compelling understanding of the priorities of the people they want to persuade.

You are persuading people every day and you must become exceptionally good at the people side of your work as well as the technical side of your work. If you don't, you will not have a seat at the executive decision-making table and will be relegated to being seen as a cost to be minimized rather than a profit to be maximized. How can you secure a seat at the executive decision-making table? How can you persuade others more powerfully, enhance your leadership brand and reputation, and be seen as a strategic value creator? Here are seven persuasion strategies that require you to use your ears first before opening your mouth.

1. Speak the Other Person's Language

In order to root out the important and strategic objectives of the person you're trying to persuade, this is the basic blocking and tackling required of all professionals. You must know how the person you're working with prefers you communicate with them. Do they prefer you provide lots of data with a historical perspective? Or do they prefer you to get to the bottom line and give them an executive summary? Do they want you to ask them questions and involve them in a conversation? Or do they want you to tell them what to do and just get things done? If you use the wrong language with a key decision-maker you'll frustrate them, lose credibility, and waste time and energy.

2. Focus on Their Self-Interests Not Yours

Every person you interact with has an unspoken list of self-interests that influence their behavior. Some people are influenced by accuracy and perfection and others are interested in consensus and including all of the right people. The more you listen to people and learn firsthand what's important, the more you'll be able to fulfill a person's self-interests and work to convert their desires into solutions you can provide.

3. Drop the Technobabble

Stop using acronyms. Acronyms are really helpful in providing a shortcut for communicating within certain groups or teams. However, when you use a technical acronym a client, customer, or leader doesn't know or understand you create a division between you and the other person. This is a division that erodes trust and respect and prevents you from understanding what's at stake and important. If you want to build resonance and communicate credibly, stop using technical jargon and talk in terms the other person understands.

4. Think, Act, and Talk Like a Trusted Business Advisor

Presenting solutions that you hear yes to is rooted in being thought of as a trusted business partner. This means you will have insight, experience, and perspectives that are valuable to another person. To build the receptivity to hear your ideas and partner with you on an issue requires that you listen to understand rather than listen to respond. If you listen to understand you will leave others heard and understood in powerful ways. Once someone feels heard they are significantly more receptive to listening to your recommendations and trusting what you have to say. Strategic business partners are highly adept at asking the critical business questions in the "Why Focusing on Inputs Is a Career-Limiting Move" section of the Projects Principle.

5. Know Their Driving Business Objectives

Whatever your functional role or expertise, my recommendation is counterintuitive—forget your technical expertise and instead focus on the other person's most pressing business objectives. This is hard for some technologically trained professionals because they view the world from a technological perspective. Learning how to talk in less binary or linear ways and focus more on strategic business issues and how you can help achieve business goals should be your number-one priority.

6. Fall Out of Love

Most people who enter highly technical fields have fallen in love with their technology. They love using their education and training to solve highly complex technical problems and take a great deal of personal pride in doing so. And therein lies the problem. They place more value on being a firefighter than they do on helping others become fire retardant.

Tim Chester at the University of Georgia told me, "IT departments should outsource the transactional and keep the transformative." This type of thinking leaves many technically trained people feeling uncomfortable, as it represents a sea change in how they view the value they provide. They only know how to be the hired technical pair of hands and not an advisor who creates accelerated business results. This is a death knell for most technically trained professionals.

7. Be Memorable

Every interaction throughout your day involves, impacts, and influences those with whom you work. The question is whether or not your impact and influence is positive. Your intent may be as pure as driven snow, but if your impact is negative your influence deteriorates. Technically trained professionals need to remember that if there is nothing very distinctive about their work and the value they create then they will end up extinct.

• • •

If you remember, what the human resource director wanted was clear and authoritative data. What the seven steps allow you to have is a clear and authoritative executive presence. When you add data with executive presence you have an unmatched combination.

Listening can be an art form. As with paintbrushes and paint in the hands of a gifted artist, listening can create a masterpiece that brings delight and awe to the person being listened to. In the next section I will share eight strategies to use when you do open your mouth, as opposed to the previous seven strategies that detail what to do *before* you open your mouth. The ideal way to look at the previous section is with regards to receptive persuasion and the following eight as expressive persuasion.

Handling Competing Priorities

In this section we'll talk about how to present your ideas in such a way that people will want to say yes to them. There are eight strategies for having someone say yes to your requests. Some of the strategies are more mindset-related and others are more skill set related. But in each case the strategies are a positive step forward to hearing someone say yes to your ideas.

Persuasion Strategy #1: Put Others First

Although it may seem repetitive or unnecessary, the first mindset strategy reminds us to be of service. Why do you need reminding to be of service? Because there is continuing pressure at all levels of an organization to deliver business results, sometimes at any cost. The admonition is to do more, do it better, do it faster, and do it cheaper. This mantra can, depending on how it's deployed, place results ahead of relationships, profits ahead of people, and doing ahead of being.

To be of service to another you must start by caring deeply about what is important to the person you want to persuade. This requires knowing that you have business objectives that must be accomplished, but that getting a "sale" may preclude you from getting a second, third, or fourth much more profitable sale. The only way to secure the fourth sale is to make sure the first and all subsequent sales are clearly linked to being of service to the other person and making his or her life easier or better. What specifically are their priorities and what, if any, promises have they made that you can help them achieve? Everything you accomplish will start here.

Persuasion #2: Be Open to Being Persuaded

Persuading someone to say yes to your request rests with you being persuaded also. In the 1980s when Ronald Reagan was president and Tip O'Neal was speaker of the house, both men knew that having the president's agenda make its way through the House of Representatives would only be accomplished with Tip O'Neal's approval.

Although both men were consummate politicians and negotiators, they knew that an openness to being persuaded was essential to making political progress. They were open to being persuaded, and by doing so, provided the other person with something they could live with but probably not love. What's important to remember with the Persuasion Principle is that persuading another person to your way of seeing a situation is never a black-and-white, right-or-wrong type of proposition, but more along the lines of good, better, and best.

The same holds true with securing a yes to your ideas of, say, $450,000 of added head count. If the only option is for someone to provide you with exactly $450,000 worth of additional headcount *or else*, you are likely going to be disappointed and seen as a "my way or the highway" type of leader. What is required in order to hear yes from a colleague or boss when requesting additional resources is a clear willingness to be receptive to new and possibly more resourceful ways of thinking about the allocation of resources. It is a resourcefulness that is capable of being persuaded to see your perspective differently. Rather than an "or else" mindset, cultivate a collaborative and mutually beneficial mindset.

Persuasion Strategy #3: Exude Confidence

Exuding confidence for many leaders is not a problem. The problem is that their confidence comes from their title or where their names appear on the organizational chart as opposed to the power of their ideas. When this happens their confidence is perceived as arrogance. Arrogance, an exaggerated belief in one's abilities or importance, is not attractive and repels the adoption of ideas.

Confidence, on the other hand, is rooted in certainty and belief in a position, person, or outcome. Confidence about your ideas, when coupled with a collaboration and mutually beneficial mindset, are essential for transformational leaders. If you believe in something firmly, are willing to be persuaded, and are enthused for persuading others, you've built the foundation for the next step.

Persuasion Strategy #4: Be in The Moment

Far too often we are dissociated from the present moment. We predominantly think about our past experiences with persuading others and whether or not we were successful, or we are projecting into the future and thinking about our request for additional resources and what we'll do if we're rejected. When our thinking is in the past or future we aren't listening to the person discuss his or her priorities and hopes for the future. We're interpreting him or her based on our past or our future, both of which preclude us from hearing subtle clues in voice tone and word choices. It also creates anxiety and apprehension. Coaches always say to athletes, "Get your head in the game," whenever an athlete makes a simple mistake. For transformational leaders the clarion call is to get your mindset in the moment.

Persuasion Strategy #5: Use the If/Then Strategy

When you are presenting an idea you will hear concerns, objections, or questions. This is exactly what you want. Concerns, objections, and questions show engagement whereas a flat refusal to support you shuts off any conversation. When you hear an objection such as, "My priorities are to reduce my budget by 7.5 percent while also decreasing the wait time for customers on hold regarding the new credit card promotion. I know I can do this because the one-time expenses for the closed office in Baltimore will be completed by fourth quarter, so I'll be okay there, but I do need to reduce the wait time."

The objective in using the if/then strategy is simply to continue the conversation to see if the collaboration and mutual benefit strategy can be utilized. For example, "Paula, I have an idea about how I can help you decrease the customers' on-hold time issue you have. *If* it were possible that my team, who has successfully worked on this same issue for us, could share our best practices and help you accomplish the hold time targets you want, would you *then* be willing to help me with the headcount issue I'm working on?"

Persuasion Strategy #6: The Magic of Three Yeses Strategy

If you want someone to say yes to providing you with additional resources, an important step is to provide them with three attractive options for saying yes. If you have high levels of trust and respect and a track record of exemplary results, presenting only one option has, at most, a 25 percent chance of success. Presenting only one option leaves people curious about other possibilities and a "no" becomes the easiest way to halt the process.

When you provide two options it presents a binary choice, which usually falls into the thought process of "right and wrong" or "good and bad." This also halts the process and reduces the odds of someone saying yes to your ideas to the same odds of flipping a coin—a 50/50 chance of success. Conversely, when you provide three options, all of which are capable of meeting the other person's needs, wants, or objectives, your success rate on one of your options being accepted goes up to 90 percent.

Persuasion Strategy #7: The Powerful Language Strategy

Without language we can't request that a barista make our favorite coffee; we can't make known our feelings for a partner, spouse, or child; and we can't tell the doctor where it hurts. Language is a powerful tool for good or ill, but in the world of email, Twitter, and social media it has devolved to an abridged 140-character world of the fewest possible words. Culturally, we now accept "No worries" as a response to a positive gesture as opposed to "You're welcome."

I observed two leaders in a team meeting discuss a difficult and complex issue. On three occasions, the first leader used language such as "That idea won't work" and "That's unnecessarily complex and cumbersome." The second leader used language such as "We can build on that idea by . . ." and "Your ideas are really helpful for me to think more clearly about this issue and how we can move forward faster. Thank you."

The first leader's language was rooted in what's not working and the second leader's was rooted in what can work next. The first leader was communicating a judgment that what had been extended was unacceptable and unworkable. The second communicated the opposite.

Think of the words you use as seeds planted in the fertile soil of someone's experience of you and that the response you receive to your ideas and requests are the harvest of what words you planted. The two leaders in the previous example used a different language and had a level of receptivity to their ideas that is directly proportionate to the language. As a transformational leader you should try to choose positive, uplifting, optimistic, and grateful words that are a catalyst for positive persuasion.

Persuasion Strategy #8: The Show-Me-the-Money Strategy

This strategy may invite memories of Tom Cruise yelling "Show me the money!" into the phone in the movie *Jerry Maguire*. Tom Cruise's character is a down-and-out sports agent desperate to hold onto a client and is persuaded to talk like his football star client. Money is not the answer to every persuasion dilemma you have, but recognize that many leaders in organizations are hyper-focused on driving business results and do see most of the decisions as financial decisions. If your request does not enable someone to see a clear return on investment for saying yes to your idea your will likely fall on deaf ears.

For example, a CIO client of mine was astute enough to recognize that his $179,000 investment in an organization-wide new printer, copier, and faxing system had little to do with a new printer system. Printers were neither what was important nor purchased. What was being purchased was an "accelerator of organizational priorities" that had a 10-fold return on investment. Using several of the previous strategies listed, he clearly articulated the following:

1. The cost in hours related to employee effectiveness, ease of operation/trouble-shooting, and maintenance of the current system.
2. The costs in the future to operate the new system.
3. The amount of miscommunication and document rework based on the current system.
4. The time wasted in mission critical departments due to inefficiencies and how recovering 25 percent of the time wasted was a catalyst for the accomplishment of organizational priorities.
5. How the current system was impacting the senior executive's individual departments and what increases they would individually receive.

After totaling the figures the CIO showed a value of $3,500,000, but then cut the number in half to show his concern for being conservative on the potential upside. The $1,500,000 upside after the investment of $179,000 had a net gain of $1,321,000 with a seven-fold return on each dollar spent. This presentation showed key decision-makers that this CIO was a strategic business partner to the rest of the organization—a business partner who was committed to delivering high-value results.

In this section you learned the three-part persuasion process along with detailed actions to make each step applicable to the real world. In the next section you'll take these strategies and compliment them with what is the most underused and misunderstood principle in the book: the Praising Principle.

5

The Praising Principle

The Negative Mindset That Prevents Praising

Leaders who instill in their employees a supreme confidence in their abilities have a huge competitive business advantage. Doing so requires leaders to recognize that employees' fears and uncertainties are normal—and that their primary job is to help convert employees' fears into courageous next steps with praise and purification. Eliminating a leader's negative mindset is an essential first step in the Praising Principle, as it precedes effectively addressing the reasons why employees don't live up to their full potential.

In all of my work with executives and entrepreneurs the biggest inhibitor I've found to effective praising and, in turn, higher performance is not the skill set of the individual, but rather their mindset. In the fast-paced world of work today, the fastest way to transformational results is to cultivate the right mindset by planting the thinking that allows you to flourish while eliminating the thinking that holds you back. We'll cover this more in the calendar grooming section, but suffice it to say that there are three primary mindset inhibitors that keep leaders from praising others as well as themselves. Addressing these three negative mindsets fosters more praising and purifies the unwanted and limiting aspects of your leadership.

Holding On to the Past

The past is a powerful force, capable of propelling us toward our goals or holding us back from our potential. Unfortunately, most of us let it hold us back.

I remember speaking with a vice president of strategic projects about a project that was delayed and eventually unsuccessful. It lead to accusations and finger-pointing by everyone involved that the VP was solely responsible for the failure. Understandably, the VP felt attacked and thrown under the bus. Was he responsible? Yes, for several contributing factors, but so were the senior leaders who failed to read executive briefings and later claimed they were caught off guard when the information made it onto their radar screens. The VP looked around the executive table and saw leaders who, only days earlier, agreed with him regarding their responsibility for the failure, but remained silent as senior leaders read him the riot act.

The resentment the VP held after this meeting didn't just go away—instead, it lingered and had long-term adverse effects on the mindset of the VP as well his department. It also infected the rest of his team and strained the working relationships between his team and other leaders.

Although the VP needs to be acutely aware of the political and cultural nuances of leading within the organization, what's equally important is not carrying the past around like an anvil. What this VP needed was to reframe the past event and reclaim his most desirable future in context of the cultural implications.

Being Your Own Worst Critic

During annual reviews, leaders and employees might hear 10 accolades about their performance throughout the last year and one area for improvement. More than 80 percent of my clients tell me that, when all is said and done, they focus on the one area for improvement and dismiss what they've done well. This is similar to driving with one foot on the accelerator and the other on the brakes. That is not a strategy for accelerated performance. In fact, it guarantees reduced performance and decreases a person's level of satisfaction and effectiveness.

The dilemma is that every person listens to two mental radio stations on a daily basis. The first station broadcasts positive and affirming messages such as, "You're really talented. You're exceptionally good at taking complex ideas and making them practical and applicable." The other station isn't nearly as pleasant to listen to. "Who do you think you are? You can't do that. You're not half as good as you think you are." Whichever station you listen to influences powerfully the message you broadcast to others. And there lies the rub. Unfortunately, this second radio station gets far more airtime than the first. It also broadcasts at a much higher volume. In fact, we're so accustomed to listening to the negative broadcast in our minds that thinking positively of ourselves is considered boastful and arrogant. If we feel that way about ourselves, think about the implications for our messages to employees and customers.

Of course, that couldn't be further from the truth. Beating yourself up doesn't do anybody any good. You have the capacity to be your biggest advocate or your biggest critic. Every day, you wake up and make the choice. Which radio station are you tuning into? If you're tuning into the negative radio station playing in your head, it is time to change the station. By taking stock of what you pay attention to on a daily basis, you can determine whether the negative or positive messages get more air time. If you're listening to your biggest critic more than your biggest advocate, then it's clear you need to make a change. The good news is that once you commit to shifting your focus from negative perspectives to positive ones, you'll begin to create a different experience for yourself—as well as for those around you. You'll provide greater praise and recognition by tuning your mindset to what's working. As an executive, it is your responsibility to make sure that your mindset is tuned into the right radio station and that you then broadcast your mindset to others.

Living in Fear

Far too many of us live in fear when it comes to our business lives. For some of us, it's financial fear. For others, it's emotional. No matter the source or type of fear, fear has a debilitating effect on personal and professional growth over extended periods of time. Fear can be a catalyst for action, but accelerated progress can never be made beneath the shadow of a fearful mindset.

Some people say that fear can be a positive element in our lives. That may be true when it comes to having a healthy dose of caution against overtly risky behavior. But in the business world, letting fear take control is paramount to self-sabotage. When we're fearful, we play not to lose instead of playing to win.

Consider for a moment what would happen if you lived your life without fear or trepidation. What if you focused your emotional energy on taking proactive approaches to challenges and creating powerful solutions to problems at work and at home? Shedding the anxiety of a fearful mindset is a freeing and empowering act.

In the business world, performance decreases as fear increases. If performance is decreasing for you or your team, I guarantee that some sort of fear is behind it and the amount of praise and finding what's working is plummeting. The fear might take the form of anxiety about a new job or responsibility. It could also be financial fear of budget cuts or lack of resources. Either way, this mindset contributes to a loss of progress in the organization.

The best way to fight fear is to identify what causes it. If you can determine the cause of fear, you can redirect it and make it less frightening for you and your team. Throughout my extensive work with executives as a coach and mentor, I have discovered eight types of fear that are most common to executives. Which ones are challenging to you?

1. Fear of holding people accountable.
2. Fear of making mistakes.
3. Fear of leaving a job that sucks the energy out of you.
4. Fear of not being seen as smart and successful.
5. Fear of upsetting your boss or senior leaders.
6. Fear of turning away from current successes in order to have even greater success.
7. Fear of investing in one's self.
8. Fear of making decisions.

Each of these negative thinking habits inhibits a leader from praising effectively. In turn, what employees hear is a litany of areas for improvement without a corresponding recitation of what is going well. This one-sided narrative is discouraging and leads to underperformance and a drain of top talent.

Where Seldom Is Heard a Discouraging Word

Praise helps people feel valued, heard, and appreciated. People who feel valued, heard, and appreciated work with more passion, experiment, take risks, and grow at rates far greater than those who don't. That concludes my prepared remarks. It's likely you will have questions, so let me put some meat on these bones.

In every organization there are pockets of employee potential lying dormant. Every leader I've worked with believes that his or her employees are capable of accomplishing more than they are. When you ask employees if they could do more the resounding answer is yes. What's fascinating is that when you ask employees why they don't accomplish more or what they are capable of accomplishing the number-one answer is because they choose not to. They could if they wanted to, they just choose not to. The ability to do more but choosing not to is a massive drain on performance. Why don't people perform to their full potential? There are six reasons.

1. No Payoff

People don't perform to their full potential when there is no payoff for working to their full potential. Every leader, team, and individual employee looks for a payoff to doing their work. It could be a deeper sense of satisfaction, success, of making a difference. However you slice and dice it, human beings are meaning-making machines, and while at work we make meaning of our work. Is it meaningful, rewarding, and valuable? Are my efforts appreciated and recognized? When they're not, the payoff devolves to simply getting a paycheck. And money has been proven to not be the greatest of motivators.

2. Uninspiring Leadership

The word *inspire* comes from the Latin *inspire*, which means "to breathe life into something." When there is no life in a leader's leadership, when she is going through the motions and espousing the mission, vision, and values but not living them, employees are left feeling uninspired. Without question, uninspired leaders cannot create inspired employees unless the inspiration is to jettison themselves from the company as soon as possible.

3. Underperformance Is Tolerated

People don't perform to their full potential when underperformance is tolerated and there is no accountability. Yes, even in the face of the corporate mantra of "do more, do it better, do it faster, and do it cheaper," underperformance is tolerated when a leader turns a blind eye to his inability to learn, grow, and change, yet expects and demands employees learn, grow, and change. Also, people don't perform to their full potential when they look around and see leaders and other employees underperforming without any consequences. The message sent is clear and compelling: If you underperform, behave poorly or unethically, miss deadlines, or lose a big client you may not have your hand slapped.

4. Unclear Expectations

People don't perform to their full potential when the expectations are unclear. Leaders who don't have the bandwidth or white space to think clearly create more confusion and ambiguity than they intend. When a leader says, "I want you to handle the Cramer project," the same issue that I've found on three continents, seven countries, and 43 states is that the word *handle* is not clear. What does *handle* mean to the leader and what does *handle* mean to the employee? When leaders are clear about the results desired, the time-frame demands, the responsibilities, roles, authority, there is *clarity*. I have built a thriving advisory firm around the word *clarity*.

5. No Trust or Respect

People don't perform to their full potential when their coworkers and leaders don't do what they say they'll do and/or don't have the talent or skill to do their job well. Trust is about a person's reliability and respect is about talent and skill. When an employee or leader loses respect and trust with another person, the relationship is toast, as is the possibility of accelerated performance.

6. No Investment in Employee Development

People don't perform to their full potential when the investments in improved mindset and skill set are delayed or eliminated. The absolute fastest way to dramatically grow a leader's leadership and the results is by working with a leadership coach. Although that may sound self-serving, I too have grown at an accelerated pace because my coach and mentor is an objective observer of my work and can provide me with new ideas, perspectives, insights, and tactics for accelerated performance that I would never have found on my own.

• • •

These six reasons people don't perform to their full potential can be addressed in powerful and substantive ways. In the Praising Principle you will learn how to praise people in concrete, sincere, and timely ways so that you can affirm the opposite of the eight previous reasons, and instead create the nine reasons why people choose to perform to their highest potential.

You'll also learn that praising has a cousin skill called "purification." And much like a water filter that eliminates impurities and makes our drinking water safe, you too will purify the aspects of your leadership that detract from accomplishing your purpose, promises, and projects.

By learning how to praise and purify your leadership you will build the confidence employees have of themselves as well as of your leadership. You will encourage experimentation, risk-taking, and learning while also infusing hope and optimism into the workplace. You will, in no uncertain terms, bring out the best in others as well as yourself.

Jettisoning Judgment and Cultivating Courage and Curiosity

Every Sunday across America there are close to 350,000 raving fans who ply themselves into the stadium of their favorite football team and another 20,000,000 million watching on television. Those in the stadiums cheer ferociously, fist pump, high five, and scream their vocal chords raw whenever their teams do something they see as beneficial to winning the game. They do so to demoralize the opposition, propel their team to victory, and reward the Herculean efforts by the sport's most elite talent. You can, for the first time, attend an event with a friend and find a normally subdued person go through a Jekyll and Hyde conversion when sports are involved.

Why is it that the same executive who screams and high fives total strangers shows up at work and only gives polite applause when the team does something equally beneficial? Is it because sporting events watched with 60,000 other people release a primal passion? Is it because the emotional response is lost in the throngs of other half-crazed enthusiastic fans? Whichever reason holds true, I contend that leaders who bring an enthusiastic recognition and praise for their work teams to work will propel their teams to victory, squelch the opposition, and reward the Herculean effort some employees exhibit to getting the work done.

I'm not advocating sports-centric high fives with accompanying screaming. What I'm advocating for is a praising mindset that rewards the expression of beneficial passion, innovation, and growth. For that to be true, there are three aspects of praise that need to be present.

1. **Sincere Praise.** Praise that is mechanical, obligatory, and/or delivered in a rote manner will degrade a leader's credibility. It will be seen as artificial and contrived, and foster a relationship gap between the person giving the praise and the person receiving it.
2. **Timely Praise.** The most potent form of praise is the type that is delivered in real time. Catching employees or coworkers doing something noteworthy and commenting on it immediately raises the well-being not only of the person receiving the praise, but creates a culture in which appreciation and continued growth become strategic assets.
3. **Specific Praise.** Generalized praise such as, "Good job!" pales in comparison to specific praise such as, "Your project management work on the Carson project was incredibly

helpful. You lived out our strategic goal of improving our customer experience and let the client feel confident and at ease with your performance. They said they loved working with us. That was really good work."

The Benefits of Praise

Praise will act as a catalyst for even higher levels of success when the three praise aspects are present. Employees and coworkers know if a leader is paying attention to what they're doing and sincere praise creates a positive feedback loop in which what gets noticed and rewarded gets magnified.

Praising is also not reserved solely for employees. Leaders benefit from reviewing their own personal leadership and identifying what they have done well and what they deserve to be praised for. This is akin to the "putting on your own oxygen mask first" theory.

Although the benefits of praise are significant, to maximally reap those benefits, praise must be balanced with providing both positive and constructive feedback. This is the second aspect of praising called *purification* and we'll cover it in the next chapter. For now, it's important for leaders to recognize that some leaders may feel that praise is not necessary and that quality work is evidence of expectations met. For those of you uncomfortable giving praise or those who see it as overblown and unnecessary consider this: Employees who have been recently praised are more engaged in their work, demonstrate increased productivity, score higher customer satisfaction rates, and hold better safety records. The benefits of praise are significant.

To better develop this critical skill, it's important for you to identify how you view praise. On a scale of 1 to 10, with 1 being "don't agree" and 10 being "strongly agree," rate yourself on the following praising dimensions:

1. I am comfortable giving sincere, timely, and specific praise and recognition to an employee, colleague, or coworker.
2. I am continually on the lookout for opportunities and ways to recognize the contributions of people I work with.
3. I am seen as someone who repeatedly shows appreciation for work that is valuable and noteworthy.
4. I purposefully find ways to link individual accomplishments to departmental and/or organizational purpose, priorities, and promises.
5. I actively look for ways to instill confidence, hope, and optimism in a person's ability to do transformational work.
6. I enjoy finding ways to celebrate individual or team success.
7. I listen with the intent of understanding and not simply of responding.

If you and I were sitting across from one another I would ask to hear the scores you gave yourself and then ask you the following questions:

- Which of the seven dimensions did you rate yourself the highest and why?
- Which of the seven praising dimensions did you rate yourself the lowest and why?
- What observations or insights do you have from your responses?
- Which of the seven praising dimensions would you like to increase dramatically?

The praising assessment is not a pass or fail, right or wrong type of assessment. It is a check-in as to how you view praise and whether you have an opportunity to be the catalyst for the mindset that can propel you and your team forward. To that end, however you rated yourself, there are 11 recommendations for how to increase your effectiveness in using praise as a strategic asset. Based on your answers to the praising assessment, the following recommendations will help you improve your praising skills.

Praising With Sincerity

1. If you appreciate someone, tell them why what they did was important to you. Tell them about how what they've done is instrumental to the organization and its results, but personalize the praise by sharing the value you

experienced. When it comes to praise, making it personal is what people receiving praise see as the most important. The million-dollar question is: "How did the act that you're giving me praise for help or benefit you?"

2. Always praise with the intent of encouraging the person because that is exactly what praising does. Praising is not about checking a task off your to-do list. Praise is about helping someone see themselves as valuable and appreciated. It was noted that Abraham Lincoln believed the best outcome from a conversation was not to have the person leave the conversation thinking highly of him, but rather the person leave the conversation feeling good about him- or herself. Praise infuses self-confidence and a belief in what's possible.

3. Link your praising to your purpose and understand why it is important to you. If you cannot link what someone has done to why you feel it is important, it becomes intellectual or artificial. Make the link and you'll be not only more sincere, but also eager to deliver the praise as it's aligned with what is most important to you.

4. Remember that the praise you deliver is planted in the fertile soil of a person's memory, takes root, and grows either positive or negative beliefs. Your praise can be nourishment in a

sometimes starved-for-appreciation corporate culture. There are few evil, wicked, bad, and nasty people walking the halls of your organization, but there are people who are overwhelmed and cannot see clearly to extend a word of encouragement because their proverbial praising gas tank is empty.

Before you move on to read the section on timeliness, take two minutes to identify three people (employees, colleagues, leaders) who did something valuable and beneficial. Plan on speaking with them within the next 72 hours and extend the praise they deserve with sincerity.

Praising With Timeliness

1. In order for your praise to be timely you need to pay attention. Timeliness is rooted in being in the moment and being on the lookout for people doing work that matters. Yes, you are likely running from one meeting to another and have 200 emails screaming for your attention, but keep in mind that the people who matter most to you are continually looking at you and taking cues from your behavior. If you're not known for paying attention and seeing in real time what's taking place in your organization you'll miss

out on becoming a magnet for finding people doing good work and multiplying it.

2. Timeliness is a praising multiplier. Timeliness intensifies and multiplies the impact of praising. If you receive praise four weeks after you did something noteworthy the praise will be important, but when delivered quickly the praise is triggered in memories that are fresh. This intensifies the effects of the praise and makes it more visceral.

3. Do not rely on your memory. The longer the time between your observation of a noteworthy event and the recounting or praising of the event, the fewer the details and specifics you'll have. You'll also lose some of the enthusiasm as time clouds your feelings as well as your memories.

TIMELINESS APPLICATION

1. Think about the previous day. Did you experience something praiseworthy? If so, what was it? What can you say to that person tomorrow to communicate the value you perceived? When will you say it? Be specific.

2. Think about the last week or month and identify one missed opportunity to praise someone. What was the outcome of missing this opportunity to praise the person? What

would you do differently? What might the outcome have been if you had praised?

Praising With Specificity

1. Always share the "why" behind your praise. Communicate the reasons why what the person did is important to you, the customer, an important project, or fellow employees. The greater the specificity, the greater the impact. Think of praise as a laser beam that you direct to cutting through the busyness of the day and to target the purpose, promises, or priorities most important to you.

2. Link the praise you are giving to the individual's hopes, dreams, or aspirations for his or her professional or personal life. This requires that you as a leader know what is important to the person, but when you do, the specificity of your praise can be more rewarding for the person and more satisfying for you to deliver. For example, "Janet, I know you asked to have an opportunity to lead a team on strategic projects. Your work today confirms I need to help you find that opportunity soon. When you presented to the executive team the project scope and results they loved your clear communication and conviction. The

executive team was encouraged and excited. That's exactly what we're looking for in our team leaders. Let's earmark time to discuss more fully what opportunities are available and which one might be right for you."

3. Link your praise to continual learning, growth, and innovation. A colleague of mine, Brian Walter, once told me that he uses a "valuemercial" idea with his clients. A "valuemercial" is similar to a commercial of 30 seconds but instead focuses on the value most important to a team or organization. For example, using the previous example with Janet, a leader might start or end a team meeting with the following message: "Before we get started, I wanted to let everyone know that Janet did an outstanding job presenting the project to the executive team yesterday. What made the presentation so compelling was her explanation of the value customers, employees, and our bottom line will receive. It was sharp, crisp, clear, and compelling. I'd like you to show her some love when you see her and then let's take 20 minutes at our next meeting and review what specifically she did that made her presentation successful. It's important for all of us to be that clear, crisp, and compelling, and we can learn from Janet. Okay, now back to our agenda."

4. Praise is fuel for transformational growth both for you as a leader and for your team. The recommendations here can have a positive impact on your leadership if you implement them with sincerity, timelines, and specificity. Let's look at the opposite side of the coin. In the next section you'll learn about the purification process.

Your Life Is a Statue of David and You Are Michelangelo

In our work thus far, we reviewed the affirming and rewarding aspects of praising employees, colleagues, or coworkers doing meaningful and valuable work. Now we shift our perspective and invert the praising process. This compliment to praising is purification; its purpose is to help us identify areas that are negatively impacting performance while building our credibility as leaders. Purification is about removing obstacles and barriers to higher performance, both for the leader as well as for the employees and colleagues she or he works with.

Transformational leaders isolate one or two harmful beliefs or behaviors and work to eliminate or remove them. Although the act of praising ensures forward progress with hope and optimism, purification is frequently associated with faith traditions and involves fasting as part of a spiritual practice. Fasting provides devotees with an opportunity to turn away from the earthly and human aspects of their day-to-day existence and reflects more on the greater questions of the tenets of their faith. Purification from a medical and health perspective involves fasting as a way of detoxifying the body from impurities and toxins found in our environment and, in some cases, the foods we eat.

In this book, purification helps leaders turn away from the exigency of day-to-day work and consider the greater questions of leadership. By doing so, we detoxify any leadership impurities that may be limiting performance. When viewed in the larger context of transformational leadership, purification will help you accomplish three things: You will see leadership as never being a solo activity; you will see how becoming genuinely curious about the ways our leadership impacts those we work with can transform our leadership; and you will identify something that doesn't support your purpose, promises, or priorities. These three accomplishments change your behavior in ways that allow you to get a more appropriate result.

In this section, you will learn how best to purify your leadership as well as the leadership and performance of others. To do so there are three key factors required of you for the purification process to produce positive results.

1. Embrace purification with curiosity over judgment.
2. Strive for new insights and discernment.
3. Leverage the one-percent rule.

The purification process encourages leaders to become especially curious about the aspects of their leadership that no longer serve them well. It is not simply a matter of finding fault and punishing oneself. Judgment retards creative problem-solving while curiosity is a healthy aspect of goal-setting and seeking improvement. In a similar fashion to the Praising Principle, the Purification Assessment is an excellent tool for determining how you view purification. On a scale of 1 to 10, with 1 being "don't agree" and 10 being "strongly agree," rate yourself on the following praising dimensions:

1. I challenge commonly held beliefs and assumptions about growth and performance.
2. I regularly ask myself how I can improve what I do and how I do it.
3. I consistently look to people outside my current organization to learn and grow from them.
4. I am comfortable articulating a connection between individual growth and departmental and/or organizational growth.
5. I frequently start conversations about what great work looks like and how to do it.
6. I enjoy finding new and better ways of serving my customer.
7. I frequently learn more from my mistakes than I do from my successes.

As you did in the previous section, which of the seven dimensions did you rate yourself the highest and why? Which of the seven purification dimensions did you rate yourself the lowest and why? What observations or insights did you learn from your responses? Which of the seven purification dimensions would you like to increase dramatically?

Please remember: The assessments here are not pass or fail, right or wrong. They are best viewed as a conversation-starter for you to determine how you view purification and whether you do something to move you and your team forward. This is very similar to when Michaelangelo created his statue of David. He said in order to create a masterpiece like David he started by removing everything that didn't fit his image of what David would be. You are called to do the same. Taken together with your answers to the purification assessment, the following recommendations will help you think about how to start applying the purification process.

Purifying With Curiosity

1. Remember: Every human being does what they do for a reason. We don't know what that reason is most of the time, and until we do, we can't make sense of the behaviors we see. This process requires curiosity as to what we see and why, as well as jettisoning judgment. Without curiosity we can't look at confusing situations and earnestly try and make sense of them, and with judgment we are too

frequently putting people and situations in neat and tidy boxes that, although expedient, are generalizations and stereotypes.

2. Stop, look, and ask higher-quality questions. By changing the quality of the questions you ask yourself as well as others the quality of your answer goes up appreciably. For example, a higher-quality question is: "I have the utmost respect for Bill, but was extremely harsh in my criticism of his work on the Summit Group proposal. I wonder why I said what I did in the team meeting?" A lower-level question is: "Why did I say such a stupid thing in the team meeting?" One stems from curiosity and the other from judgment.

3. Be nice to yourself. When you use the purification principle, talk to yourself about purification in the same way you would to a friend you care about. Recognize that there are times for consolation and times for tough love and that most people are their own worst critics and judge themselves harshly. When that happens, the ability to ask higher-quality questions all but disappears and inserted into the conversation is the drill sergeant from hell that wants nothing more than to assure your self-destruction. Don't allow that person in your life.

Purifying for Insight and Discernment

1. Lighten up. Recommendation number one is: Don't take yourself so seriously. Although you want to improve and live out your purpose more fully, refrain from becoming morosely fixated on your shortcomings. The ability to see yourself clearly is an incredibly important aspect of your leadership; your credibility is important and needs to be viewed seriously. But so is the ability to laugh at yourself and your mistakes. When you laugh at yourself and your mistakes you give people the ability to more closely look at their own mistakes and take the corrective action necessary to minimize them.

2. Purification takes discipline. Insight and discernment are derived from disciplines and require continual practice. When you follow an exercise program, the more you exercise the easier it becomes. The same holds true for both praising and purifying. The more you do both the more you build into your muscle memory the process of purposefully taking an inventory of your assets and liabilities. If you want to be a more effective leader, teammate, or employee, know your strengths and blind-spots are accelerated with the Praising Principle.

3. Slow down. To gain new insights and have greater discernment, you cannot travel through the process at excessive speeds. And you especially cannot gain insight and discernment if you are multi-tasking. Mario Andretti, famed Formula One driver once said, "If everything feels as though it's under control you're simply not going fast enough." That is pithy and true in Formula One racing in one respect. The drivers are hurtling themselves around a track at full-throttle, but they also have to slow down and take pit stops. If they didn't, they'd run out of gas and be stranded on the track. You too need to slow down at times—not permanently, but frequently enough to get your bearings in order to go faster.

4. Look for patterns. We all have patterns for doing routine work. We may drive to the office the same way as well as dress and get ready for work the same way. This is a way of taking the mundane and making it more efficient. We each have only so much mental fuel in our days for making decisions and being effective. The less energy our brain uses on mundane issues the more we have for the big stuff. Are there patterns affecting you? Are you in so many meetings you don't have time to eat? Are you ruminating at night about work and only sleeping four hours? Has your

exercise program suffered because of your ankle injury and in turn you are carrying more stress and anxiety? What patterns can you see in yourself as well as with others? Be discerning as to what is causing the pattern.

Purifying With the One-Percent Rule

1. Take one day at a time. The one-percent rule posits that getting better in any endeavor by one percent daily results in a 100-percent improvement in 72 days. (In this example, I'm using the power of compound interest. So as you build on your successes each day you're accelerating to the 100-percent destination with multiplication versus addition.) The idea of getting better by 1 percent is appealing to most of my clients, as they see it as workable through finding one new idea, one new perspective, or listening to a colleague discuss what they did to improve the customer experience. Through any means necessary, transformational leaders look to get better by 1 percent each day.

2. Focus on progress. If you are a brain surgeon and you have just sawed a hole in my head I want you to be perfect in your work. Please come to work rested and please don't have an argument with your partner before arriving

in my operating room. Today is the day to be perfect. For all of you who are not brain surgeons, the other 99.95 percent reading this book, progress is preferable to perfection. I've listened to every role and job in all different organizations, and they tell me their work must be perfect. I will agree that if you are a nurse, an accountant, or an engineer working on the latest airplane, I want to know you are continuing to make progress and you've done your work correctly. But I would never ask for perfection. It's not possible, nor should you strive for it. Perfectionism leads to procrastination. Making progress leads to acceleration.

3. Narrow your focus. In the Promises Principle we talked about the number of priorities a leader can realistically have individually. I've found the magic number to be three. When you narrow your focus to the three most critical things you are committed to doing, the quality of your focus, the clarity of your thinking, and the quality of your results goes up. When you engage in the purification aspects of transformational leadership, choose your priorities and drive them a mile. You'll feel more satisfied and successful, which will be cascaded throughout your organization.

In the calendar grooming section coming up next, you'll learn a simple five-minute process for taking what you've learned in the Praising Principle and making it real-world and actionable.

Saying No to Others While Never Accepting No for an Answer

The shortest section in this chapter may have the longest shelf life. The calendar grooming process is an ultra-short (five minute) process of reviewing your day as a transformational leader. It is a process of finding the areas of your leadership that are going well and accentuating them, along with the areas that are not going well and reducing or eliminating them. Calendar grooming is similar to dressing for work every day. You remove the clothes worn to bed, shower, and put on clean clothes appropriate for the day ahead. If you have no client or customer meetings you may wears khaki pants or jeans. If customer meetings are on your schedule you may wear dress slacks and a sport coat. In either case, you look at your day and decide the best way to dress for the day ahead.

The same holds true for the calendar grooming process except the grooming doesn't happen in the morning, it happens at the end of the day and takes less time than it does for you to drink your first cup of coffee or tea in the morning. There are two versions and three simple steps to calendar grooming. The first version is an abridged yet powerful daily check-in that involves taking five minutes to answer the five questions. Version two involves taking 20 to 30 minutes once per week and once per month to review your previous observations and discern more targeted and powerful next steps. The power in version two comes from the data points you have as well as the addition of more questions. But first, here are the five questions.

1. Where was I most successful today in living out my purpose, priorities, or promises?
2. What allowed me to be successful? Be specific.
3. Where was I unsuccessful today in living out my purpose, promises, or priorities?
4. What insights can I glean about what allowed me to be unsuccessful? Be specific.
5. What is the one thing I will implement tomorrow in order to use the above insights to my advantage?

If you do this daily for 90 days you will have invested 450 minutes out of the 129,600 minutes you have. That's .003 percent of the minutes allocated to you. But you're asleep for one third of that. So you only have 86,400 minutes. That means you'll have invested .005 percent of your time. This is a fraction of the time you have available, but like the parable of the mustard seed moving mountains, calendar grooming can, with the mindset of passion, innovation, and growth, move the mountain that is your leadership in satisfying and successful ways.

So, what's different in version two? Version two requires two additional steps and two additional questions. You should earmark 30 minutes during the weekend to review your calendar in totality. Think of it as the end of a quarter of play in your favorite sport. In hindsight, what went well when you think of the week as a whole as opposed to individual days? You'll ask yourself the same questions as you did all week, but with one small shift. You ask about "this week" as opposed to "today."

The main purpose is to see your week holistically and in totality as opposed to an individual day. In doing so, you will raise your gaze from the exigencies of your days and see with a broader perspective. You will expand your peripheral vision and see around the corner of your week and think with more clarity about what you want next week.

Let me talk for a moment to all of my hard-charging type A personalities who have a bias for proactive and immediate action. I know you are a doer and can easily rally yourself for action, and in many ways you have an admirable "Yes, I can, yes, I will" mindset. I want you on my team because of who you are and how you go about doing things.

But, and this will seem counterintuitive, if you want to go faster, for five minutes go slower. If you groom your calendar you will move the needle on key issues with greater effectiveness. By taking five minutes each day to answer these questions through the prism of praising and purifying, your actions and the actions of those you work with will become laser-focused and allow you to accelerate toward your destination. Give me .005 of your time and I'll prove it.

6

The Perseverance Principle

Talent Is as Common as Table Salt and Can Ruin Your Dinner

I've met exceptionally smart and talented leaders who, when confronted with adversity, crumble like a house of cards in a windstorm. I've also met other leaders whose talent and brilliance is less pronounced, but who will persevere through unimaginable adversity in order to be successful. After all of my coaching and consulting work I've concluded that when it comes to transformational performance, talent is overrated and perseverance is underestimated.

Perseverance is prominently displayed in the world of politics, business, and sports. In politics, Abraham Lincoln failed to be elected or reelected 12 times before finally being elected President of the United States. Sir Eric Dyson experimented 5,127 times in five years to develop his cyclone vacuum cleaner and now has a net worth of five billion pounds. Dallas Mavericks basketball team owner and multi-billionaire Mark Cuban was known for working until 2 a.m. and not taking a vacation for seven years. And then there are the talented athletes who were not expected to become the mega stars they are because of talent or stature. Think of Michael Jordon, Serena Williams, Russell Wilson, and Wayne Gretzky. Are they talented? Absolutely. Were they or are they currently the hardest-working athlete in their sport? Absolutely.

Each of these athletes was born with gifts and talents, but without a disciplined work ethic and perseverance their gifts and talents would never have reached the potential they did. Russell Wilson is too short to play in the NFL, but he won a Super Bowl in this first three years because of a mindset of "My 2016 goal is just to win. Win in everything I participate in." Wayne Gretzky was the right height and weight for a hockey player and he had good instincts. But his instincts were honed from an immense number of hours on the ice. Serena Williams once said about success, "Luck has nothing to do with it, because I have spent many, many hours, countless hours, on the court working for my one moment in time, not knowing when it would come."

Of all the principles we've covered so far the Perseverance Principle is where the rubber meets the road. It's the principle that asks "How badly do I want my purpose? Will I overcome all the obstacles that will surely come? Will I not take no for an answer? Will I look through the fear of failure that will likely show up and be courageous anyway?" My contention is that when you articulate a big idea, hope, dream, or aspiration, you feel passionate about your perseverance.

The War for Talent

The term "war for talent" has been bandied about for the last two decades. It is an admonition to executives and entrepreneurs that no matter what great idea, product, or service you have, the achievement of your strategic goals will only happen when you have the right talent. Yes, talent is an essential element in all leaders' success, as success is never a solo activity.

If you are like many of the leaders I work with, you have talented employees who lack the perseverance necessary to overcome adversity. You may have recruited the best talent and skill set, but neglected to recruit the best mindset. A hospital CEO I know recruited one of the most prominent surgeons in the state. His talent was exceptional as was his love of his craft. What was equally exceptional was his disdain for collaboration with colleagues. His mindset was one of "I'm the best surgeon in this specialty on all the eastern coast." Although true, his belief about his talent and repute as an exemplary specialty surgeon left others seeking medical care of their own. Yes, talent is important, but equally important is what happens in between the ears of each person.

Your job as a transformational leader is to recognize that talent, although essential, pales in comparison to perseverance. Yes, you want to have talented, smart, gifted employees on your team. You also want to look around the room and know that the talent you have will run through the teeth of battle if need be to accomplish strategic initiatives. You can help them do that first and foremost with a compelling purpose. You too will never achieve transformational results without deep reserves of grit and determination. In the sections that follow, you'll learn how to persevere in the face of adversity and how to overcome the four barriers to doing your best work.

There are no easy magic bullet steps, however. What you'll find is that the muscle you need to train more than any other is the muscle resting on your shoulders and in between your ears. In the next section you'll learn strategies for doing just that.

Why Winston Churchill's Advice to Schoolboys Applies to Adults

Perseverance is an interesting principle. The concept of perseverance is well known and of late has been studied and dissected and laid at the feet of how we were raised. Did we learn positive impulse control as children? I personally did not learn impulse control as a child. At 12 years old, my family doctor said the reason for my inattentiveness at school was rooted in ADD. That may have been true, but there were areas of my young life that fascinated me and that I would get lost in. I persevered immensely in subjects I was interested and engaged in, and relegated the traditional subjects to the scrap heap.

In many ways I learned perseverance in counterintuitive ways and am glad I did.

Winston Churchill once addressed his school and talked about the last 10 months of World War II for Britain. He said Britain had been rejected by its allies to join in the war effort and was waging a war against Germany alone. He said, "But for everyone, surely, what we have gone through in this period—I am addressing myself to the school—surely from this period of 10 months this is the lesson: never give in, never give in, never, never, never, never—in nothing, great or small, large or petty—never give in except to convictions of honour and good sense."

But, how do you never give in? Is it through force of will or is there a magic bullet? I don't believe in sheer force of will or magic bullets, but I do believe in processes. The process I use is the same process many professional athletes use and is proven to increase your perseverance significantly. It's called the "The Giddy-Up Process" and requires you to answer nine questions:

1. **What do you want?** Answering this question is the jumping-off point for perseverance. Think back to the Purpose Principle. What is the big idea you have in mind for your personal and professional life? Does it fire you up? Does it inspire you? You will not persevere if you have a fuzzy idea about what you want. There are millions of people walking around who have a vague notion of what they

want. But not you. With crystal-clear focus, describe what you want.

2. **What's important about that to you?** Throughout the Projects Principle as well as the Persuading Principle, I urged you to ask the question, "What's important about that to you?" That question is now being asked of you. If you want a promotion to the VP of Sales position, what's important about that to you? Keep in mind that your answers have to inspire you and light a fire underneath you. If you follow each of the principles and want to be rewarded with a promotion to the VP of Sales position, what's the payoff for you, your organization, your employees, and your customers? If your answers are uninspiring and what you want and are doing are out of obligation, that becomes a long, slow slog through enemy territory. It will drain you and ensure your failure.

3. **What will you need to give up?** Make no mistake about it; what you want will require that you stop something. It may mean you'll have to stop work at 6 p.m. and be home to have dinner with the family. It may require you to stop employing people you like, and instead employ people who are comfortable never rating the bar on their performance. It may require that you jettison the negative mindset

you carry around and the corresponding need to please others. What are the top three or five things you'll have to give up? List them and look at them in black and white.

4. **What will you need to learn to be successful?** If you need to give up being liked or decide you need to learn how to set the bar higher for you and your team, where will you learn how to do that? The tension you will always feel is the pull back to what is known and predictable and away from the desired yet unpredictable future. What book, class, or webinar will you take in order to learn how to do something?

5. **Who will you need to surround yourself with?** In parallel to the last question, who will you surround yourself with? There is a minuscule chance you will be successful in persevering if you are surrounded by people who want the opposite of what you want. For many recovering addicts there is a time period in which they cannot spend time with friends or family members who drink or use drugs. The pull to their using days is so strong that they have to surround themselves with people who are, as they say in the recovery movement, "working." That is, working the process and on the same journey. You too need people who believe in you and will support you in your grand journey.

6. **What story will you tell yourself every day?**
There are two stories being told every day
inside our heads: the story of "Yes, we can" and
the story of "No, we can't." These two stories
become the way we perceive the world around
us. It is not the car that pulls out in front of you
that frustrates you. It's the story you tell yourself about the moron who needs to have his
license revoked because of his inept driving.
This stupid person of course cannot be known,
but that's the story we tell. We also tell similar
stories about ourselves. What is the dominant
thought you will carry with you as you move
toward your purpose, priorities, and promises?

7. **What will you do when adversity hits?** If you
have lived on the Gulf of Mexico for 20 years
and are told by the Weather Service that a hur-
ricane is headed to your end of the beach and
will make land fall in 12 hours with winds of
85 miles per hour, you will have been though
hurricanes before and will have mapped out a
process for handling danger such as this.

The same holds true for perseverance.
If you know the obstacle you will face, for
example, I buy junk food when I shop hungry, you can make plans for not going to the
grocery store hungry. If you know that not
sleeping well makes you resistant to your
teams' ideas for process improvements, you

can plan on going to bed earlier before big team meetings or can develop a process for vetting ideas for process improvement that does the heavy lifting for you.

8. **How will you reward yourself?** Far too often leaders believe that perseverance is the price of entry for being in the world of work. No matter what, get your job done through thick and thin. That is true in one sense. As a leader you are required to overcome adversity and get big projects done whether you're on fire about the project or not. But on the other hand, if your work is continually asking you to over perform without any reward, you are headed for a flaming burnout and a massive amount of resentment. If you think about your purpose and the corresponding priorities and promises, what will you do to reward yourself for engaging in a stretch leadership project and being successful? A special dinner with a loved one? A new pen? A new sport coat or piece of clothing you've admired? If you don't have a reward there is a tendency to become a martyr or become resentful.

9. **Who is your exemplar?** When I'm at my best with perseverance I have a mental picture of someone who is the epitome of what I want to accomplish. I may know the person or may have only read about them. Having an exemplar

also helps with the story I tell myself. My mentor Alan Weiss is one of my exemplars. His zest for life is one of his most compelling traits. He savors life and scoops up as many new experiences as possible. He loves the theater, traveling, wine, food, challenging conversations, reading, exploring new ideas, and helping people like me fulfill all of my potential.

For you to persevere in all of the important areas of your life you need to answer these nine questions. Just think back over the last three months either personally or professionally. Which of these nine questions, if answered fully, would have been beneficial for you? If perseverance and sticking to your goals and aspirations are important to you, take five minutes to read this list again and answer the question in ways that clarify your thinking and focus your attention. When you do, the fog will lift as to what you need to do to persevere and you'll accelerate toward your destination with gusto and conviction. In the next section, we'll discuss the two primary ways you will approach success for you and learn how to play to your strengths with perseverance.

The Tortoise and the Hare in Organizations

The tortoise is not well thought of in the world of work. If the choice is between the slower, more deliberate and methodical tortoise and the rocket-fast but solitary and not persevering hare, most leaders prefer the hare. Why? Speed is vitally important to every business today. Customers expect hare-fast responses to their questions and when they receive tortoise-like responses the impression is that the business doesn't care. What follows a business's tortoise-like response is a hare-quick post to social media about the slow response.

How quickly does your business respond to shifts in the market or to customer complaints? When you see a process inside your organization that needs revamping, do you think about it for prolonged periods or do you hare-fast rework it? The reality is that the tortoise and hare responses are both valuable, just in different contexts. For example, there are initiatives that can be and need to be implemented in hare-fast time frames. There are also initiatives that can only be accomplished with what feels like plodding progress. For example, the personal mastery process doesn't come blisteringly fast. You can make quick gains early in the transformational leadership process, but radical transformations come only after long periods of what is seen as mind-numbing effort with little or no progress.

The Benefits of a Tortoise and a Hare

Since I am not advocating for the hiring of either long-eared, herbivorous, fast-running hares or a land-dwelling reptile, let's be clear about the tortoise and the hare metaphor. The tortoise represents that part of our work and professional lives that can only be accomplished with perseverance and a protective outer shell. The destination is clear and in focus, but it comes forward in baby steps. The hare represents the fast-twitch muscles required to get out of the blocks fast, but that cannot be sustained over long periods of time. You need both capabilities but will remain transactional in your benefits if you try and have employees do both. That is similar to asking a 350-pound offensive lineman to play wide receiver on a football team.

In order for you to achieve your purpose, promises, and priorities you need to value the benefits and limitations of both the tortoise and the hare. You need to build a protective outer shell to the naysayers and those who will suggest you slow down and not push so hard. You will have to embrace running at full tilt without having all the answers to what seems like mission-critical questions. Winston Churchill embraced both the tortoise and the hare ways of working when he admonished his cabinet that negotiating with Hitler, even in the face of nonstop bombing and the death of British citizens, was futile. He also implored his cabinet members that success was achieved through the rapid deployment of new armaments. He did so while Germany had successfully invaded France and British troops were encircled at Dunkirk. Some may say he was incapable of being persuaded, but in essence Churchill knew that victory for Britain, however perilous, was not a one-pronged strategy, but a two-pronged tortoise and hare strategy.

Three Steps to Building an Impervious Outer Shell to Detractors

Seek Respect, Not Friendship

My mentor Alan Weiss once told me that if I wanted to be liked that I should get a dog. As an advisor to executives and entrepreneurs my focus should be on being respected. Alan has a witty and penetrating way of cutting to the chase. In the early part of my career doing business reorganizations and turnarounds I spent an inordinate amount of time trying to be liked as well as respected. In my role I had to make hard and difficult decisions and sought to make them in ways that would preserve my good standing with the people affected. It didn't work. I worked harder and under greater stress because I needed to be liked. As an immigrant and someone who had moved numerous times during the formative years of my life, I unknowingly was trying to avoid being rejected while also being respected. The freedom I have known comes not from trying to be all things to all people, but rather to be the person who exemplifies my purpose, and is ruthless with keeping promises and works to create transformational value for my clients.

Ask for Advice, Not Feedback

I learned an important lesson about the difference between advice and feedback. When I asked for feedback, people were all too willing to provide it, but I didn't have an interest in whether it was helpful or actionable. And oftentimes, I learned that the feedback I received was geared more toward preserving the self-worth and self-esteem of the person giving the feedback. I've found that my desire for success oftentimes shadows others' desire and consequently the feedback from others with a differing view of success is rooted in having me be less successful.

Transformational leaders ask for advice instead. Feedback doesn't require action once the feedback is given. It is too often a one-way transaction in which the person giving the feedback sees their responsibility ending with the shared feedback. Advice, on the other, hand is shared between two colleagues who respect one another and who want the best for one other. Advice, when asked for sincerely, generates a substantially different response than feedback. Advice includes a desire on the other person's part to partner with the person and advise them about how to achieve their purpose or desired state. Advice is seldom thrown over the transom, but rather handed personally to the other person.

Court Your Purpose

The third way to be impervious to detractors is to court your purpose out of hiding and into the daylight of your everyday life. In the Purpose Principle the word *love* was used to describe one of the essential building blocks of your purpose. When you fall in love with your purpose you will treat it in a similar way as how you treated the early loves in your personal life. You will write notes of affection; you'll spend time with the person and tell them all the things you like and admire about them. You act in ways that, in retrospect, may seem sappy and adolescent, but was rooted purely in how you felt toward the other person. You were impervious to the rational part of your mind, and were moved by the love toward the other person.

The same holds true for your purpose. Treat it with the care and love you would a person you love. Serenade them with words of affection and care, spend time enjoying their company, shower them with gifts that show your appreciation, and know that each day you feed your purpose the stronger it grows and the more of an inseparable bond is created.

Two Steps to Building Hare-Like Reflexes

Become Improvisational

I spoke with an executive today about his inability to execute as fast as he wanted to. He knew the technical aspects of his work through and through, but was stumped as to why he was faltering with execution. What I heard in the 20 minutes we talked was his high need for every action and response on his part to be right. He had set up in his thinking that, when right, he would be successful. When he was wrong he would be a failure. He had painted himself into a corner and, in turn, had imposed on others the same requirement. Wrong actions or decisions were, in his thinking, unacceptable. This belief slowed him and his team down substantially. At the root of the issue was a high level of self-criticism. He held himself to an exceptionally high standard and whenever the standard was at risk of not being met he did what he felt was required in order to be right, and unknowingly communicated to his team the same high standard he had for himself along with the criticism.

Although you may think this requires a therapist to resolve, I beg to differ. What I've seen with smart and intelligent executives is that the moment they see the fallacy of their thinking they move naturally toward fixing it. We discussed using three steps to being more improvisational. The first is to shift the thinking from black-and-white, right-and-wrong thinking to the good, better, and best thinking. For example, a good answer may not be his ideal answer, but it's good in that it creates a starting point for creating a better answer, which, if followed by experimentation and risk-taking, can lead to the best answer. We also discussed how improvisation is high art and requires wicked smart wits and can be developed over time. This line of thinking resonated with him as he saw this as intellectually appealing. He also agreed to watch, listen, and catch himself being critical of himself and others and to identify when he does it and under what circumstances. The more light he can bring to this aspect of his leadership, the more improvisational he will become.

Build Muscle Memory

I've been a runner for most of my life. A sprinter by training and experience, I enjoy the thrill of full-throttle running. It's hard for me to run in a group and not to want
to speed up and overtake the person up front, but when
I started doing triathlons the sprinter in me learned the
hard way that my muscles needed to adapt to long, slow
swimming, biking, and running, and that completing
was the objective—not competing.

Experts in triathlons taught me that my muscles
could adapt and that I could infuse sprinting into my
triathlons, but only after months and years of persistent
training. Once my muscles had learned both the sprinting and extended duration aspects of a triathlon, I could
choose the appropriate approach to swimming, biking,
and running at the appropriate time. When you want to
run like a hare you cannot go out and in one day become
hare-like. It takes time and a process of gradually and
purposefully increasing the load on your muscles to
handle the increasing demands. For example, which is
more comfortable for you? The tortoise or hare way of
working? If the tortoise, decide to decrease the amount
of time it takes you to do the least attractive part of your
job by 25 percent. If you prefer the hare way of working, which area of your leadership do you see as taking
way too long to accomplish? Who is the one person who
you trust and respect that you can go and ask for advice
about how to benefit from working with the tortoise?

Whichever skill set you want to develop, recognize that when a purpose has grabbed hold of you and has you fired up about accomplishing it, there is an unwavering spirit that encircles you. You wake up in the morning visualizing your day and how you will enthusiastically exemplify your purpose. You go through your day actively finding ways of infusing your purpose into your voicemails, emails, and meetings. When you think of your critical decisions that need to be made you have your purpose operating in the foreground.

But in order to persevere and achieve transformational results for yourself, and before you can assist others in doing the same, you have to recognize that you cannot be a 350-pound offensive lineman as well as a wide receiver simultaneously. You have a perseverance DNA, a talent, skill, and preference for one type of action over another. But you can become impervious to naysayers and obstacles by following these steps. In the next section we'll discuss the four obstacles to doing your best work and integrate the learnings from this section to the next.

The Four Barriers to Doing Your Best Work

Without question, every transformational leader wants to do compelling and meaningful work, and they see their leadership purpose as the starting point for doing so. Yet with every starting point comes a slowing point that can, if left unattended, lead to a stopping point. Leaders who are successful and satisfied have learned how to address the four most common barriers that inhibit them from accomplishing their purpose. By understanding these leadership barriers, leaders are better prepared to overcome the barriers and lead purposefully rather than accidentally.

1. Inertia

Inertia is seductive. It is easy to get lulled into doing your work and leading the work of others in the same ways you have always done it, even if it doesn't work anymore. Every person on the planet knows that change is certain and that growth is optional, yet the appeal to remaining the same is appealing because it doesn't require change and the accompanying discomfort of learning something new. Inertia infects us with a virus that multiplies the acceptance of replicating the past even in the face of knowingly doing uninspired and pedestrian work. Ask 10 leaders if their work is inspired, creative, transformational, innovative, and purposeful, and the affirmative responses will be in the one-to-two people range. Ask also the same 10 leaders if they honestly would describe their work as lacking creativity and producing safe and predictable results, and you'll hear the affirmative six to eight times. How is this possible? Quite simply, as we discussed in the Promises Principle, when leaders have 12 priorities and feel overwhelmed, overworked, and overburdened, the likelihood of them devoting more energy, time, and resources to reinventing work is almost non-existent. They've become Sisyphus simply waiting for the end-of-the-day boulder to roll down the hill and squash them. They've given up and resigned themselves to their current state of affairs.

What is astounding, however, is that when leaders find their one hope, dream, or idea that's grabbed hold of them, when they see their way to cull the herd of their priorities, when they stop trying to correct their weaknesses and instead play to their strengths, it's curtain time for inertia. It doesn't mean that life becomes butterflies, ice cream, and unicorns, but it does mean the mindset of the leader is transformed and so are their beliefs as to what is possible.

2. Ignorance

You can be smart and ignorant simultaneously. For example, a leader can be technically brilliant, well-educated, have a brilliant and compelling work history, and remain ignorant about an employee's or customer's hopes, dreams, and aspirations.

I also believe it is a safe assumption for me to view those of you reading this book as well-intentioned, smart, and talented leaders. I don't think you are broken, nor do I see you as a slothful ignoramus. What I do see in every boardroom, cubicle, and corner office are leaders who are either not informed or ill-informed about the power of purpose, who have become addicted to using hard facts and data to lead themselves and their organizations; I see leaders who have forgotten that their behaviors are impacting their performances and that capturing the hearts and minds of employees is job number one. They are smart, don't get me wrong. But they are smart about all things other than what's required to create the organization transformation they so desperately want. They're ignorant about the people and relationship side of leadership.

Throughout this book you have been introduced to strategies for winning back your heart and mind as well as the hearts and minds of those you lead. In one sense, you are no longer ignorant about the art and science of leadership, but ignorant about what barrier is most holding you back. Is it truly that you don't know how, or have you been ensnared by inertia and haven't found the exit door? Before you answer what's ensnared you let's talk about the next barrier, incompetence.

3. Inexperience

Inexperience in a transformational leadership context is not as severe an indictment as it sounds. It doesn't pertain to the long-term ability of a leader, but instead is an observation about the short-term talents and skills needed to do transformational work. Inexperience applies to new or more senior leaders who are fully capable of learning how to perform meaningful work, but who lack the specific, targeted, and current skill set to become a transformational leader. Inexperience points more to the opportunity for skill development, both for leaders as well as their direct reports.

It might be easy for you to say, "Yes, my team is inexperienced and I want to develop a more innovative, passionate, and growth-focused mindset." It might be easy to clarify the skills required to handle an upset customer or retain a customer who called to close their account. But the transformational leader is continually asking themselves what new experiences and education they need to lead the transformation they envision. Do you need more experience leading based on purpose? Do you need more experience about crafting your leadership promises and priorities? How about persuading others or leading strategic projects? If your answer is that there are no new experiences or education you need, can I remind you to reread the ignorance and inertia section again? If not, you'll want to listen for the roar of the heavy boulder rolling down the hall toward you.

4. Indifference

Nine times out of 10, indifference comes from not having a clear and compelling leadership and/or organizational purpose. For some leaders, achieving financial results is their purpose. This purpose, however, does little to win the hearts and minds of employees or customers. Yes, achieving financial results is essential to remaining relevant, but financial metrics as a purpose counterintuitively ensures lower performance. What transformational leaders recognize is that making a meaningful difference in a person's life jettisons indifference and brings forth greater creativity, energy, and a willingness to change and grow.

I've seen indifference come in many different forms. There is the indifference that comes from inept senior leaders, unrelenting budget cuts, contentious contract negotiations, disgruntled customers, sales, marketing and operations misalignments, product quality mismanagement, and a personal life that is out of control. I've also seen it rooted in simple things, such as poor health, poor sleep, and poor nutrition.

The times in which indifference comes from someone who truly just doesn't give one iota about the product, customer, performance, reputation, or well-being of a coworker of colleague, the indifference needs to be rooted out and treated like a cancer. If it's left to its own devices it will metastasize and kill you or your organization. This is where transformational leaders step up. They will not allow the inertia, inexperience, or ignorance to deter them. They will be on a mission to remove indifference the moment it raises its head.

Every principle you have learned about so far is required to overcome these four barriers to doing your best work and for creating a culture in which others come to do their best work. Although there are times that removing the cancer of indifference may require an immediate and radical procedure, most often what's required is perseverance in the face of adversity. In the next section, you'll learn how to leverage both the tortoise and hare ways of approaching work and create transformational results.

Why Execution Trumps Strategy

In the vocabulary of the Perseverance Principle, execution trumps strategy for three primary reasons, each of which is rooted in outdated and incorrect perceptions about strategy. These perceptions, when seen as a whole, point emphatically to the importance of thinking strategically about your leadership, your business, your employees, your results, and your sense of personal satisfaction and success. However, they also point to the game-changing reality that strategic thinking, if not married to ruthless execution, is destined to fill up yet another shelf of highly thought of but rarely used binders of strategic plans. Look at your bookshelf—either on your computer or a physical bookshelf—and ask yourself one question: If I were to grade me, my team, and my organization on the ability to convert strategic ideas into actionable, profitable, and rewarding results, what score would I give on a 1 to 10 scale? In this situation, 1 is deplorable and 10 is exemplary. What follows are the most important and relevant misperceptions about strategy and execution.

Outdated Perception #1: Strategy Is a Respite From a Busy Day

The first incorrect perception most people hold is that strategy sessions are a way to tune out the exigencies of the day and engage in intellectually stimulating, sometimes fun, energizing conversations. Although you may get energized by strategy, the best perception to hold of strategy is that it is a rigorous process of self-examination about prior results, what worked and didn't work, and what the demands facing you and your organization are. Strategy sessions are simply a launching pad for doing work that will improve your business position. It is essential that you answer questions such as "Where will we as an organization be in two to three years?," "How will we make a meaningful difference in our customer's life?," or "What do we want our employees to experience and achieve in two to three years?" These are engaging and important questions and, for many people, enjoyable because they are transported away from the harsh reality of today's priorities. Strategy sessions allow them to imagine a future full of new possibilities—new possibilities that may very well be more enticing than the current state of affairs.

New Perception: Strategy sessions are a staging area for accelerated performance. Period. Yes, having a clear picture of your future is essential, and yes, being passionate about your future is required, but the stage needs to be set that, in order to persevere in achieving your future state, the persistent and consistent execution required is what needs to be clearly in mind moving forward.

Outdated Perception #2: Successful Execution Eliminates Failure

In the world of work many people have come to the conclusion that they have to be successful in every endeavor they undertake. Success therefore requires eliminating failure, as failure is not tolerated in many organizations. The stakes are too high, the investments too large, and the customer too finicky. Yes, winning the war is required, but to think for a moment that the war can be won without losing a battle or two along the way is foolhardy.

The most negative and misplaced perception I encounter in my work is the one that states: If you fail, you will be relegated to the district office in Fargo, North Dakota, and your career path will be significantly limited. This type of thinking means that many leaders come to execution tentatively. They are hesitant to execute because if they execute incorrectly they will be seen in a less favorable light.

New Perception: Infuse into your leadership the belief in F3: *Failing Forward Faster.* Persevering in the face of adversity is assisted when examples of leaders and individuals who have achieved noteworthy results are front and center. Remember the examples of Sir James Dyson, Oprah Winfrey, Babe Ruth, J.K. Rowling, Thomas Edison, and Abraham Lincoln. Inculcate into your meetings and leadership that if you are not failing, you are not trying anything new. Perseverance is an intellectual construct and not a value to be exemplified.

Outdated Perception #3: Speed Is Dangerous

In the world of automobile racing speed is the name of the game. The person who can go around the track the fastest and cross the finish line ahead of their competitors is the winner. Race-car drivers in turn go the fastest they can by being right on the edge of speed and safety. They are not afraid of going fast. As a matter of fact, they are continually looking for ways to go faster, not in foolish or reckless ways, but in ways that are right on the edge. Spectators may find motorsports exhilarating to watch, but when given the opportunity to experience the speed of automobile racing up close and personal, the spectator squeals like a 5 year old who just saw a mouse in her bedroom.

And yet, speed is the new currency in the world of work. The amount of $10 million can be transferred from one financial institution to another in the click of a mouse. Customer perceptions can change in an instant if an employee's reaction time to a problem or issue is too slow. But far too many employees fear speed because they see speed as reckless, imperfect, and undesirable. They feel this way because they are metaphorically driving on the racetrack of work, not in a Formula One racing care, but in the family minivan. You too would feel out of control racing in a minivan.

New Perception: Redefine speed as dangerous only if the vehicle and racetrack you are driving on are mismatched. Discuss what new skill set, mindset, equipment, processes, and systems are required to decrease the time to market for new products or increase the response time for key customers. Have a bias for consistent and persistent action. Redefine what the costs are for slower speed and what the payoffs are for faster speed.

• • •

Perseverance and execution trump strategy because strategy is fine and good in that it sets direction for you, your team, and even your organization. But the reality is that achieving your strategy requires a perseverance that is best described as ruthless and unrelenting.

In this chapter you've likely found one or two areas that point directly to the barriers holding you back from your most important strategic initiatives. The tough-love part of transformational leadership is this: Until you fall in love with your purpose and want it with such ferocity, the perseverance described here is simply words on a page. When your purpose grabs hold of you and won't let go, the words on this page are no longer intellectual constructs floating around in your head, but rather ideas that compel you to lace up your running shoes and move your feet. The next section is about converting everything you've read into a final plan for being a catalyst for transformational results.

7

The Preparation Principle

Living a Purposeful Life Versus an Accidental Life

Although I advocate for being purposeful in every area of your life, there are events and times when you will not and cannot be fully prepared. On December 13, 2016, my family experienced a disaster that no one wanted nor were we prepared for. My brother-in-law, Joey Sharron, was swimming in Mexico when two waves hit him from behind and pushed him head-first into a sand bar. His neck was broken on impact and were it not for a woman standing on the beach 25 yards away and yelling for her husband to help him, he likely would have drowned and been pronounced dead at the scene.

He received 15 minutes of CPR without being resuscitated. As the lifeguards were stopping CPR, a physician from an adjacent hotel, who had watched the accident, ran for a defibrillator, and arrived on the scene and started CPR again. His arrival and intervention lasted 10 additional minutes and, after administering four shocks, he revived Joey.

Emergency surgery was performed in Mexico and three days later Joey was transported to Mass General in Boston where he was diagnosed as a quadriplegic. He is alive, has no brain damage, and has an amazing mindset. He is, in many ways, preparing himself and his family to accept his prognosis merely as a starting point, not his finishing point.

Two weeks into Joey's injury I'm not fully prepared to grasp the enormity of his injury or the impact this will have on each family member. There are aspects of caring for and living with an accident of this magnitude that is beyond comprehension and leaves each of us crying and ill-prepared to deal with the severity of his condition.

But in the face of this accident, Joey specifically, and my family in general, have learned something new each and every day about what's possible—possible for his recovery, possible for his work, and possible for what we can do to make the healing process healthier. Watching Joey handle this adversity in inspiring and courageous ways tells me that Joey can teach me a lot about the Preparation Principle and Transformational Leadership. Joey has said that he's never going to give up and that he knows exactly what's going to be thrown at him physically and emotionally. He knows this is a massive test for his health and quality of life, but also for his wife, family, and business too. He's not naive in any way, but he believes that how he thinks about his injury and by the choices he makes with his mindset and his rehabilitation, he can overcome the situation and lead a productive and healthy life. Joey's attitude is transforming what I believed was possible and is preparing me to be amazed at what he accomplishes.

The title of this section is living a purposeful life and not an accidental life. *Accidental* doesn't mean accidental in the sense Joey experienced or that your leadership and life are mere accidents. But what I find with every executive and entrepreneur I've ever worked with is that the demands of their work are inhibiting them from designing the leadership and life that allows them to flourish.

The reality is that your transformational leadership journey will be filled with obstacles and barriers you anticipated as well as those you didn't. You've likely looked at aspects of your leadership as well as your organization's performance and realized much of the work you are doing needs to be transformed. You may have looked at your customer experiences and seen where they need to be transformed, or that your employee experiences need to be transformed in order for them to be able to bring their best selves to work. By now, you might be saying to yourself that your work needs to be converted from a long, slow slog in enemy territory with bullets flying over your head, into the highest expression of what you hope for as a leader.

One executive I worked with repeatedly told me of the eight to 10 meetings they were in each day, and the

250 emails they received. There was no white space to slow down and think, and they lamented that they felt like a *human doing* as opposed to a *human being.*

There are times when it is the nature of the beast to go from meeting to meeting and to navigate a mountain of emails. But the risk in doing so for prolonged periods of time is that you end up convincing yourself that you're doing your best work. That would be similar to thinking that you could run a marathon every week for 52 weeks and expect for the 13th marathon to be as strong and powerful as the first, or that the 52nd would hold the potential for a personal best. That's twisted thinking.

Whatever transformation you want for your organization, it will always start with you preparing for and undergoing an individual transformation *first.* There is no way to get around that. And here in the Preparation Principle, I want to prepare you not only for the flourishing leadership transformation that's possible, but more importantly, for the personal transformation that leaves you and those who are important to you successful as well as supremely satisfied.

In order for you to cut the time it takes you to achieve greater success in half, you'll need to be prepared to address the realities of transformational leadership. Specifically, you'll need to learn to: welcome barriers and obstacles; be the role model for what you envision; leave the safe, comfortable, known, and predictable; and prepare for greatness and learn from a 16th-century monk. Let's cover each one in more detail.

Your Greatest Barriers and Obstacles are the Gateway to Your Greatest Successes

Your greatest successes are hidden in your greatest failures and barriers. Do you believe that? Let me make my case. Whenever you find yourself stuck or hindered from accomplishing what you want, there is a barrier or obstacle that's preventing you from greater progress and, once addressed, will allow you to accelerate toward greater success. That's a no-brainer, right? Since you likely deal with obstacles and barriers every day I'll add that what hinders you most from greater success is not the obstacle per se, but that eight out of 10 times the barriers you encounter are mindset—not skill set—barriers, and in turn, cultivating a mindset of passion, innovation, and growth for yourself as well as for those you lead and work with will be the catalyst for overcoming obstacles and barriers. This is the first area of leadership you need to be prepared for.

And yet, preparing yourself to achieve your greatest successes requires a new frame of reference about barriers and obstacles, a frame of reference that welcomes barriers and obstacles because they provide you with three benefits. They are:

1. Test your mettle.
2. Confirm what you do know and what you still need to learn.
3. Be a role model to others for what you hope will become commonplace.

Let's dive into each one in more detail.

Test Your Mettle

Think about the rescue of Apollo 13 in 1970. Fifty hours into their mission and 200,000 miles from Earth, something went terribly wrong. Minutes after mission control asked the crew to turn on a hydrogen and oxygen tank–stirring fan, a sound that would send chills up any person's spine was heard. A loud and unplanned bang led to fluctuations in capsule power and the firing of the spacecraft's thrusters.

The problem was a second oxygen tank explosion following a short circuit. With limited power and life-essential resources running out, the crew had to abort their planned landing on the moon and instead use the lunar module as their lifeline. Engineers were given a mandate to bring the astronauts home safely. They worked around the clock to figure out how to provide them with oxygen, power, and a plan to return to Earth.

Close to four days after that ominous bang, Apollo 13 hurtled itself around the moon and successfully splashed down on Earth. Their return was hailed as one of the world's most unprecedented engineering achievements and stunned not only the astronauts, but the world at large. This rescue was the ultimate obstacle as well as the ultimate in testing the engineering mettle of NASA. Afterward, this event role modeled what was possible and allowed, rather than the cancellation of other missions. It also allowed the continuation of the Apollo program.

It is not hyperbole to say that imbedded in every obstacle and barrier is the seed of your greatest achievement. Steve Jobs was ousted from Apple after a disagreement with cofounder Steve Wozniak. Steve Jobs never saw the oust coming and later said that getting fired from Apple was the best thing that could have ever happened to him. Jobs turned this obstacle of being kicked out of the company and focused on his Next and Pixar projects. His focus resulted in him later selling Pixar to Disney for $7.4 billion dollars. And after he returned to Apple he shepherded Apple's market capitalization from $3 billion in 1997 to $350 billion in 2011. He did not go quietly into the night, sit in a corner, and lament his lot in life. On the contrary, he threw himself into other projects and channeled his drive and energy purposefully.

Confirm What You Do Know and What You Still Need to Learn

One of the great things about obstacles and barriers is that it confirms what we do know and what we don't know and need to learn. In the NASA example, imagine a meeting with all of the engineers when they learn of the Apollo 13 disaster. I envision a meeting in which every engineer lists out what is known about the situation. They'll need oxygen, thrust (to preserve physical as well as lunar module power), and they'll need easy-to-follow instructions because of the lack of food and energy. That probably resulted in another list of what they did not know and needed to find out. What do we not know how to fix now that we need to fix first in order to make progress in bringing these astronauts home?

Obstacles are delightful in this regard. There are things in every form of adversity that you will know how to address or fix. But it will also be true that there are things you won't know how to address or fix, and that will require you to learn something new, expand your knowledge, and possibly your ability to work with diverse groups of people to come up with the best solution.

Be a Role Model to Others for What You Hope Will Become Commonplace

Leaders like you, Joey, and me are role models. People are continually watching leaders, especially in times of adversity, and take their cues as to what they should do when the road to success is blocked. When employees see a leader respond with courage, confidence, and commitment, the message is sent in ways corporate marketing or human resources departments cannot send: This is the way we as an organization or team respond.

The important insight about role modeling is this: As a role model, you should welcome being tested, because when you're tested and smack up against a yogurt-covered fan, you'll learn more and grow more than you ever imagined possible, and you'll become the exemplar for your organization as to what values and beliefs guide your leadership. If you didn't have obstacles or barriers you would never have the refining fire for your leadership or the opportunity in real time to powerfully communicate what's important to you. You would also have no urgency or desire to get better. You would be complacent and content to remain the same.

Barriers and obstacles, which you will find from doing the work I recommend, are necessary in order for you to become a transformational leader. And quite frankly, if your mindset is such that you want to avoid barriers and obstacles, your leadership becomes fat, flabby, uninspired, and, frankly, pedestrian.

Throughout the seven principles the case I'm making is this: When you find and articulate the one idea, hope, dream, or aspiration that has grabbed hold of you and won't let go, it's a game-changer. It changes how you engage at work as well as at home, it changes how you engage with employees and customers, and it changes the performance and results of your teams and organization.

But for many of you the idea of having this rallying cry for your leadership is clouded by your experience of the corporate communications department's work on mission, purpose, and vision. Once articulated and distributed within six months no one can remember it or discuss it in emotional and compelling terms, so it dies a slow and quiet death.

However, when you work through the Purpose Principle with earnestness and commitment, the clarity and focus you need to take barriers and obstacles and convert them into opportunities for greatness emerges with greater frequency. Until you have this clarity and focus for your leadership, your leadership is more intellectual and less emotional. Yes, intellect is important, but to overcome big obstacles, you and your team must care deeply about something bigger than yourself; something other than money, profit, market share, and so on. Yes, they're important, but transformational leaders are in love with something noble, uplifting, and meaningful.

In the next section we'll look at how not preparing is the death knell for your desired results and what plans you need to make to become transformational.

Leaving the Comfortable Confines of the Safe, Predictable, and Known

From time to time you'll find that what you're doing is no longer working. I have worked with technology executives for more than 10 years. One of the hardest things they have had to leave behind is their enjoyment of the technical side of their work. They entered the technology field because of an enjoyment or skill in programming and have become enamored with programming or the intricacies of their technology. Although loving what you do and being good at it is essential to success at work, they've lost sight of the business value technology brings to an organization. When I suggest they forget their technology and instead focus on the business and economic value to their technology, I'm rewarded with deer-in-the-headlights looks. You would have thought I asked them to put their first child up for adoption. The separation anxiety they experience is rooted in the carefully constructed value they ascribe to themselves. If they're an expert in their technology they will be seen as valuable and successful. When I ask them to focus on business and economic value to technology investments they don't know how to do that, have never learned how to calculate ROI on technology spending, and experience the fight, freeze, or flee response. Importantly, until they know how to do what I'm asking, and until they see the value in doing so, they remain stuck in the known, safe, and predictable.

The same holds true in healthcare. Several of my hospital clients have physicians and nurses who can only see the world through the prism of their specialty or practice area. The implications for their practice areas on the overall businesses are not considered. The same can be found in higher education where many professors never leave the safe and comfortable confines of the ivory tower to know what is truly in the best interest of the world of work students are entering.

So what's required in order to leave the safe and comfortable confines of the known and predictable? If you want to get the results you dream of, be prepared to step into the crucible that leadership is and recognize that there are four key motivators for leaving the safe, comfortable, and known.

Dreams

The clarion call for writing this book was to prompt you to think bigger about your leadership and to connect your thinking with plans that have the power to convert your work life from a job into the highest expression possible of what is most important to you. In no uncertain terms, my dream was for you to become a catalyst for human flourishing in the world of work. But that cannot happen accidentally. It can only happen purposefully when a leader is no longer satisfied or content with his or her leadership and results.

When you have a dream for your professional life there will be times when you experience high levels of dissatisfaction. Dissatisfaction is a sign that your dreams are being thwarted or are at risk of being compromised. If you are never dissatisfied with your current state or the changes taking place around you, your dreams are either too small or you have an unprecedented tolerance for maintaining the status quo. You go on a diet when you're dissatisfied with how your pants feel and when your dreams of feeling comfortable in your clothes are in jeopardy. You'll replace your car when you're dissatisfied with the upkeep of your current vehicle or a dream of driving a newer model pervades your thinking. Each of our dissatisfactions are rooted in a dream we have.

The same holds true with your leadership. What part of your leadership are you dissatisfied with? What part of your leadership do you think needs to be dreamed of differently so that you can enjoy work more and also have a bigger impact on others? Dissatisfaction is not a negative. It's the catalyst you need in order to start the process of dreaming bigger in order to leave the safe, comfortable, and known.

Choices

Each and every one of us has the capacity for floundering or flourishing. It is a choice we get to make and is ours alone. Which have you chosen today? To choose to flourish takes courage. Courage comes from the French word *coeur* and means "heart." For you to choose to step outside of the safe, known, and predictable into uncharted territory is, as Joseph Campbell said in *The Power of Myth*, a heroic choice. The dissatisfaction you may feel compels you, oftentimes reluctantly, to venture outside the known and safe and to pursue something different even in the face of not having a clearly charted path. Dissatisfaction propels us to make choices based on the full knowledge that remaining the same is no longer an option, and that making a tentative choice forward into the unknown will be supported in time with faith and courage. The journey to transformational leadership is never linear and requires all of the seven principles. Each principle can help you to be more courageous and turn away from what has made you successful in the past toward what will make you successful in the future.

Beliefs

Let's be clear: To be a transformational leader you must believe you are not a victim. You have the power and capacity to make decisions, to make plans, to learn new skills, and expand your experiences so as to be more valuable to your organization, your customers, and your employees. With very few exceptions, the senior leaders in your organization believed in something and were purposeful as to what they wanted to create either in their role, scope, or impact. The believed that what they envisioned was possible and that they were responsible for creating it.

While working with Starbucks, a senior vice president told me the story about how the founder and CEO, Howard Shultz, started working for Starbucks as a marketing manager and left four years later to start his own coffee company because of a disagreement with the owners. He believed he would be better off leaving and starting his own company. Four years later he bought the company from the original owners and now has an empire of 25,000 coffee shops across the world.

The story was told in the hopes of sharing insights as to what makes Starbucks what it is today. Starbucks is led by a CEO who believes it is better to walk away from situations that are not right and don't hold the potential for doing great work. Was there a risk for Howard Shultz to leave? Certainly. Was there a benefit? Certainly. What was present in copious amounts for Howard Shultz was a belief that living and leading a life of his choosing is never dictated by circumstance. He believed and chose to live his life in ways where he had greater control and influence and not to delegate that to others. Will all of your decisions pay as handsome a dividend for you as Howard Shultz's decision did for him? Actually, yes, they will. They will just look different.

If you dream, choose, and believe, the likelihood is that you will commit to moving outside of the safe, comfortable, and known. The commitment that's next is to continually put one foot in front of the other without wanting guarantees or to know everything will be perfect. It's about making progress every day toward that which is important and inspiring for you. That brings us to the fourth key motivator.

Action

What one idea have you learned so far that prompts you to do something different, scary, bold, or exciting? Leadership is primarily a solo activity in that no one can dream, make choices for, or believe for you. You must do all of that on your own. But once you've dreamed, made a decision, and fostered an unshakable belief, doing something each day that moves the needle on performance comes naturally. More than anything every successful leader has cultivated a bias for action—a bias for taking one action every day that gets you closer to greater success and satisfaction.

My experience is that the motivators in the shortest supply are *dream* and *belief* and the motivator that is in the greatest supply is *action*. And therein lies the dilemma for many leaders. They find themselves compelled to act but haven't clarified their dreams and by extension cultivated the belief necessary to be successful. I am not naïve, nor do I have my head in the sand when I consider the demands faced by most leaders today. The rate of change has accelerated to the point that most leaders feel dizzy, overwhelmed, overburdened, and over-scheduled.

What should you plan on doing? You should prepare yourself for a breakthrough. If you like the idea of a breakthrough in performance and what it means professionally, let me also prepare you for what precedes a breakthrough: a breakdown. It's not uncommon for breakthroughs to be preceded by breakdowns in communication, breakdowns in resource allocation, breakdowns in employee/leader trust and respect. Wherever you envision a breakthrough, attaining it requires overcoming your biggest barriers, leaving the safe and comfortable behind, and embarking on a hero's adventure. Although your breakthroughs are aided and made easier with the seven principles of transformational leadership, in the next section you'll learn a three-step process for taking the dreaming, choosing, believing, and action framework and making it relevant to your everyday work life.

Failing to Prepare Means Preparing to Fail

Is failing to prepare the death knell of transformational leadership? Yes, but not in the manner you're accustomed to. The planning I'm advocating is the planning for undergoing the individual transformation required to lead the organizational transformation you desire.

In the Purpose Principle, I claimed that defining your purpose is not the same as looking at life through rose-colored glasses. The questions about purpose, meaning, and significance are not softball questions, but rather the hardball strategic life questions my clients courageously ask themselves.

And for too many of you, the exigency of your daily to-do list forces you into a transactional way of engaging with life and leads to never planning to live the most rewarding and enriching life. It's not in the plans, so it's not going to happen.

People at work or in your personal life who have achieved something extraordinary and who live lives defined as rewarding and uplifting have a clear and compelling plan for achieving what's important to them. In this section, I want to take any theory and convert it into actionable next steps. But there is a rub: I don't believe there is a one-size-fits-all prescription for planning your leadership. Yes, the seven principles have existed for millennia and have transformed cultures both positively as well as negatively. What I am convinced of, beyond a shadow of a doubt, is that once you have a leadership process you believe in and you have a purpose that is compelling for you, you are smart enough and talented enough to make a decisive plan for your leadership.

So, in this chapter I am not taking the position of the sage on the stage handing you stone tablets with 10 strategies for leading the organizational transformation you want. Instead, I'm respecting your intelligence and commitment and acting as the guide by your side. As a fellow traveler and guide to executives and entrepreneurs on the road to flourishing, I will share with you what my most successful clients (and possibly Howard Shultz as well) have done to plan for personal and organizational transformations. In turn, you'll have a prescription for next steps you can personalize in ways that work for you.

The Preparation Principle outlines specifically what successful leaders do above and beyond the other six principles. The following three characteristics of transformational leaders are continuously planned into the daily work of leading their organizations.

Transformational Leaders Wake Up

The first thing transformational leaders plan on doing is waking up. Not in the sense of opening their eyes first thing in the morning and getting out of bed, which of course they do, but they wake up to their hopes, dreams, and aspirations, they wake up to the impact they have on others, they wake up to what they do well, why they don't do well, and what they will do to get better. Waking up in this sense is the process of continually looking at the activities, actions, and mindset the leader has in seeing themselves clearly through the eyes of the people who matter most to them.

They wake up to the reaction others have to their emails, voicemails, and the meetings they hold. They are also waking up and seeing clearly what their triggers and vices are. For example, they wake up to the fact that when the senior-most executive in their organizations attends one of their meetings, they become overly forceful and describe their work in grandiose and overly productive ways. Transformational leaders wake up to their impact with others as a catalyst for either greater performance or lesser performance.

Transformational Leaders Grow Up

When transformational leaders grow up they take 100 percent responsibility for their actions and their impact. They don't shy away in any manner or form to the fact that they have a responsibility to positively impact those that they lead. In turn, they take 100 percent responsibility for their actions and decisions, and do so willingly. They have grown into the realization that people are continually watching them and taking cues as to what is important to them and how they should behave.

They also grow up to the fact that many employees don't like to be held accountable and that one of their primary jobs is to role model accountability and truth-telling.

This is not theoretical for transformational leaders, but is planned into their work on a daily and weekly basis.

Transformational Leaders Show Up

By showing up we're not referencing just physically being present, but mentally and emotionally present also. By showing up, transformational leaders have woken up to the priorities and promises necessary to achieve their purpose, as well as execute on their projects; they plan behaviorally specific actions that send a leadership message in purposeful and powerful ways.

Transformational leaders recognize that the only tool they have in their toolkit is themselves. That is a liberating as well as frightening thought. You are the vehicle by which one of two things happens: extraordinary performance or ordinary performance. By your actions people will know what you stand for, what you value, hope for and will reward. The showing up process is never ending for transformational leaders and frankly they don't want it to be. Transformational leaders recognize that doing transformational work is not a paint by numbers exercise nor is it a straight line point A to point B endeavor. There are circuitous routes that occasionally take leaders down dead-end roads, and while many people may think this a waste of time, the transformational leader looks at these diversions as an excellent opportunity to show up as a continual learner. A learner who aspires to innovate and grow based on their successes as well as their failures. In order for you to plan for success and satisfaction you need to continually wake up, grow up, and show up. If you don't embrace these traits and characteristics then life is a journey with accidental outcomes. The Preparation Principle and this section on planning is not about how to manage your calendar specifically, but rather strives to impress upon you that living your purpose, priorities, and promises each day is a choice you must make purposefully otherwise it will not happen. With intention and attention to your leadership as well as your personal life, your life plan is one of your designing.

In the next section we will link waking up, growing up, and showing up to what you can learn from a 16th-century monk by the name of Ignatius of Loyola.

What Can You Learn From a 16th-Century Monk?

Discernment. That's what you can learn from Saint Ignatius of Loyola. Discernment about yourself primarily, but equally as important, discernment about others and how their thoughts, words, or actions trigger a response in you. Let's be clear about something before we discuss the merits of St. Ignatius: Leadership is a solo activity in the sense that you are the only tool you have in your toolkit. Yes, I've said that before, but it's worth repeating because there is nowhere for you to hide when it comes to being seen, known, and a catalyst for transformation.

Every major faith tradition extols the benefit of knowing oneself in the pursuit of the divine. Buddha said, "It is better to conquer yourself than to win a thousand battles. Then the victory is yours. It cannot be taken from you, not by angels or by demons, heaven or hell." The Prophet Muhammad said, "He who knows himself knows His Lord." In the Bible, in Lamentations Chapter 3 verse 40, it reads, "Let us examine and probe our ways, And let us return to the LORD."

While I've stipulated that you have to undergo an individual transformation first in order to create an organizational transformation, you too will be required to lead others through their own transformation. In order for the biggest and most audacious results to be yours, you will have to know yourself in ways you don't now, and by so doing, assure the victory Buddha spoke of while probing your ways as in Lamentations. Waking up to the real you, the you that is capable of extraordinary works, may have fears and concerns rooted in whether you're capable of being transformational. If you are like the leaders I work with, waking up to what's working in your leadership and what's not can feel daunting. That's why I want to introduce you to a 16th-century Catholic monk by the name of Saint Ignatius of Loyola.

Who was Ignatius of Loyola? Loyola was a hot-headed rich kid born into nobility in 16th-century Spain. He joined the army at 17, and was known for strutting around with his cape swung open to show off his legs in tight-fitting hose and sword. He was a womanizer, had a big ego and a quick temper, that had to rely on his privileged status to escape prosecution for numerous violent crimes. At the Battle of Pamplona in 1521 he was gravely injured when a cannonball hit him in the legs, wounding his right leg and fracturing the left in multiple places. He returned home to his father's castle in Loyola, where he underwent several surgical operations to repair his legs, having the bones set and then reset when his vanity got the best of him. His vanity was such that he had his legs rebroken because he thought his legs would look bad in tights.And this was before anesthesia. Think about that for a second. The vanity and narcissism of Ignatius was profound.

But here's where the story gets interesting. Ignatius woke up to the direction his life was taking. He saw the vices, addictions, and ways of being in the world that led him away from what was good, uplifting and eternal, and toward what was selfish, narcissistic and ego driven. He underwent a spiritual conversion that led after many years to the creation of the religious order the Jesuits. Today there are 16,000-plus Jesuit priests, brothers, scholastics, and novices worldwide which represents the largest male religious order in the Catholic Church. Jesuits are pastors in parishes, teachers, and chaplains. They are also doctors, lawyers, and astronomers. They care for the whole person: body, mind, and soul and in their education ministries, they seek to nurture "men and women for others." All this came from what was an ego-driven, angry, spoiled rich kid? Yes, and what Ignatius left behind and is the central part of what is called Ignatian Spirituality is the Examination of Conscious. A 15-minute, once or twice daily, examination of the day's activities and how we respond to them.

While I personally have practiced Ignatian Spirituality for the last three years, I'm not suggesting you embrace it. What I am suggesting is that the practice Ignatius suggested is transformational in its ability to increase our awareness of ourselves and of the world we experience. When you are an overwhelmed, overburdened and over-scheduled leader you need a process for pulling back the layers of your way of seeing the work and people you interact with and infusing a transformational discernment process into your day. The variation on Ignatius's examination I'm going to propose is without a doubt the fastest way for leaders to facilitate their own individual transformation. If you use this process once per day you'll grow faster and be capable of leading others with greater clarity and focus.

Here's a snapshot of what Ignatius taught in his Examination of Conscious. There are five parts to Ignatius's process, five questions that when answered purposefully and thoughtfully takes 15 minutes to answer. They are:

1. **Creation: Where did I see God's love expressed or received today?** Ignatius believed that the whole world was created from love, in love, and for love. He helped Jesuits pay attention to all of creation as an act

of love and to intentionally and purposefully seek out examples of things created in love and for love.

2. **Presence: Where did I experience God's presence today?** Ignatius also believed that God was hiding in plain sight and that we didn't need to go looking for the Divine, but that we needed to simply be more aware of where the Divine was hiding in plain sight. This question raises our awareness to the Divine and asks for examples of where God's presence was felt or seen.

3. **Memory: What were the events today that was a violation of love done to me or by me?** This is a biggie for Ignatius. What he asked priests to do was review every moment of their day from rising from bed all the way through to going back to bed. He wanted Jesuits to become acutely aware of their affective states. For you and me, he wanted us to pay attention to the kid with his jeans hanging 12 inches off his waist, with earbuds, and slowly walking across the crosswalk oblivious to us missing our light because of him. Ignatius would want to know our reaction to him and would say to all of us today that understanding the reactions we have to situations is essential if we are going to lead a movement. We have to understand ourselves in light of our strengths as well as our shortcomings.

4. **Mercy: Where do I need God's mercy today?** We never live up fully to our potential. We fall short and disappoint people. This question was to remind people that we do have shortcomings and that we can be extended forgiveness just as we can forgive others.

5. **Eternity: What am I excited about for tomorrow and why?** This last question is rooted in the belief of creating a new heaven on earth as a co-creator with the Divine. What will I create tomorrow and what is exciting about doing so for me?

The first paragraph of this section said discernment is what you can learn from Saint Ignatius. Discernment about yourself primarily, but equally as important, discernment about others and how their thoughts, words, or actions trigger a response in you. I've created a variation of Igantius's questions but with the same intent of creating a transformational perspective of yourself and others so you can as Gandhi said, be the change you want to see in the world.

Hugh's Transformation Examination

1. Where did I create the most value and/or well-being today?

Every day you have the opportunity and responsibility to plant in the hearts and minds of your employees and customers something of value and/or well-being. Identify one, two, or three ways you created value or well being today. Over time you will see this part of your professional life more clearly, which will instill greater confidence and courage in you as well as more credibility and connection with those you are interacting with.

2. Where was I most present and in the moment today?

Far too often leaders are either living in the past and living an event from weeks, months, or even years ago. This has them living in fear of repeating this event. Or, they are living in the future to the extent that they are disconnected from the important insights and impact of the present. This question pulls you toward the current moment so as to see at what times and in what places are you most connected and present. This is a powerful clue as to what part of your work is the most captivating for you.

3. What are the two or three most pivotal events or experiences I had today and what was my reaction to them?

This part of the Transformation Examination is about getting real with yourself. It asks you to isolate two or three events from the day and specifically identify your reactions to them. This question is not a onion-peeling, navel-gazing question, but rather a massively important awareness-building question. Remember the admonishment from Socrates about Know Thyself. That's the intent of this question.

4. Where do I regret not living up to my highest potential today?

Let's be real. There are parts of the day that don't go well. We do something or say something that has a negative impact on someone or damages our reputation. When we can see these events clearly and own them we are living responsibly. Over time you might see patterns to your shortcomings, and with the help of the other principles, a coach, or mentor you can devise strategies for reducing or eliminating it. But change in this area requires seeing and owning the shortcoming. A word of caution though. This question can bring out your worst critic and can become an opportunity to scourge yourself. Avoid that by paying attention to the Praising Principle.

5. What am I excited about creating tomorrow and why?

This is the part of the examination that most people like. They are action-oriented leaders who want to get going and do some planning. Yes, it is empowering to know what you will create from one day to the next, but only when your plans for tomorrow are insightfully informed by today. Isolate two to three things you want to create and why it is important to you.

What is your reaction to these questions? Do you see them as helpful, valuable, provocative, time-wasting, navel-gazing, or an impediment to doing the work that matters most to you?

Whatever your reaction keep this in mind. These questions are not time wasters. They are performance accelerators. What the people whom you lead want most of all is to trust you, respect you, and have a meaningful personal connection with you so they can come along side of you and create something noteworthy and transformational. They want that from you, but you cannot give that to them unless you trust, respect, and have a personal connection with yourself. The Transformation Examination will help you build the connection and by doing so, transform your leadership as well as create a mindset of innovation and growth.

All throughout this chapter I've presented you with options for how to prepare for the leadership adventure before you. Each strategy for preparation is assisted with the Transformation Examination. In the closing section I'll sit down across from you with a cup of coffee and suggest how to integrate all of the principles and set you on the path to personal and organizational transformation.

CONCLUSION

So what you do you do now? That's a fabulous question and one that I do not take lightly. If you and I were sitting across from one another having a cup of coffee and I had the opportunity to share what I think are the most valuable words of wisdom I can share, here's what I'd say.

Remember that if you're not flourishing individually the likelihood of you enabling employees or customers to flourish is incredibly small. Just as it is with airline safety announcements, you need to put on our own oxygen mask first. I would tell you to put your oxygen mask on first and make a promise to choose to flourish personally. Take the Purpose Principle and drive the concepts there a mile. Find just one idea, hope, dream, or aspiration and grab hold of it and don't ever let go.

I would tell you to make a decision. Make a decision about your priorities and the promises that you'll make to the people who matter most to you. I would tell you that the promises and priorities you make define you as a person and are the backbone of character. I would remind you that they are directly linked to what you articulate in the Purpose Principle, and that you are far more capable of choosing each and every day what the quality of your life will look like. You are not a victim, nor are you in control of the entire universe, but you have an amazing life, so choose carefully each and every day.

Focus on value creation. Forget your methodology, forget what you do technically, and live, breathe, and do everything you can to understand your customer's experience. I'd remind you that what matters most is making peoples' lives easier. When you do that, not only will your employees' and your customers' lives be more rewarding, but so will yours.

Remember that in every single meeting, email, or other interaction, you have an opportunity to persuade someone to support you, and have them embrace employee and customer flourishing. I'd look you square in the eyes and remind you that you make a difference in peoples' lives and that you should accept that responsibility fully and with enthusiasm because, with your purpose, your promises, priorities, learning, and growth, you can create a community of like-minded co-conspirators who do amazing work.

I'd ask you to be a catalyst for community and connection where you purposefully help people cultivate the mindset of what's working as opposed to what's not working. Infuse your insights from the Praising Principle into every hour of your day, and by purposefully helping people feel good about themselves; you'll infuse hope and optimism into their work life, allowing them to flourish. I'd ask you to become the exemplar of hope, optimism, and praise.

I would also tell you to never give up. There is work that only you can do and that your work world needs you more than ever to hold true to what you find noble and uplifting. Never lose sight of that. In every corner of your organization, people are paying attention to what you do and say in the face of unrelenting adversity— adversity that can leave you drained and disenchanted. Continually and purposefully put one foot in front of the other. Your talent is important, but your perseverance is the real game-changer.

I'd also advise focusing on the Preparation Principle. The discernment and wisdom that you have within you about your leadership, your relationship with the people that matter most to you, and the impact that you're having in all areas of your life, are accelerated with the Transformation Examination. The Preparation Principle is the hub of transformational leadership and all the other principles extend from that. You need to prepare yourself to go on a transformational journey and, at the end of that journey, be prepared to review that journey and reinvent it in any way, shape, manner, or form that works for you. As I've said, you get to choose how you want to live your life both personally as well as professionally.

And the last thing I would say to you is this: Love is the most transformational emotion that you and I have. Love propels us and it changes us. So fall in love with an idea, hope, dream, or aspiration, fall in love with your employees and your customers, fall in love with doing valuable work, fall in love with infusing hope and optimism wherever you go, fall in love with praising people for doing their best work, and fall in love with the pain and discomfort of moving forward in times of overwhelming adversity. And I'd also say fall in love with the notion that each and every day can be a day filled with personal and professional flourishing. The world needs more people on fire with human flourishing. Are you on board?

INDEX

Index

ABOUT THE AUTHOR

Hugh Blane is the president of Claris Consulting. He is the globally recognized performance expert hired to help organizations solve challenging business issues, strengthen personal and professional relationships, and execute strategic initiatives faster and more reliably. His clients include Sony Pictures, Starbucks, Nordstrom, Microsoft, Pepperdine University, KPMG, and Costco. He publishes a top blog on leadership and mindset at *www.clarisconsulting.net* and is an in-demand speaker.